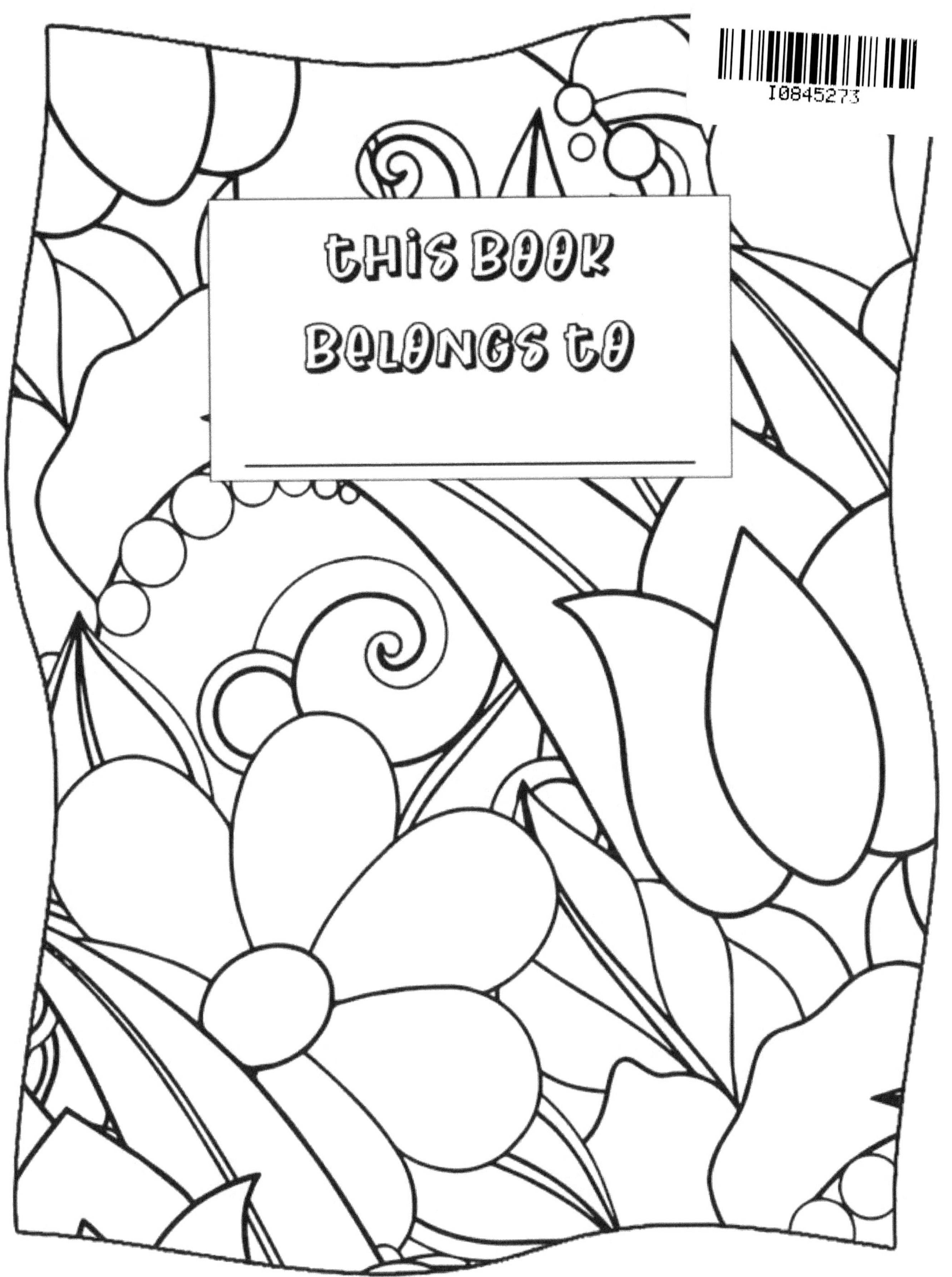

tHiS BOOK
BeLONGS tO

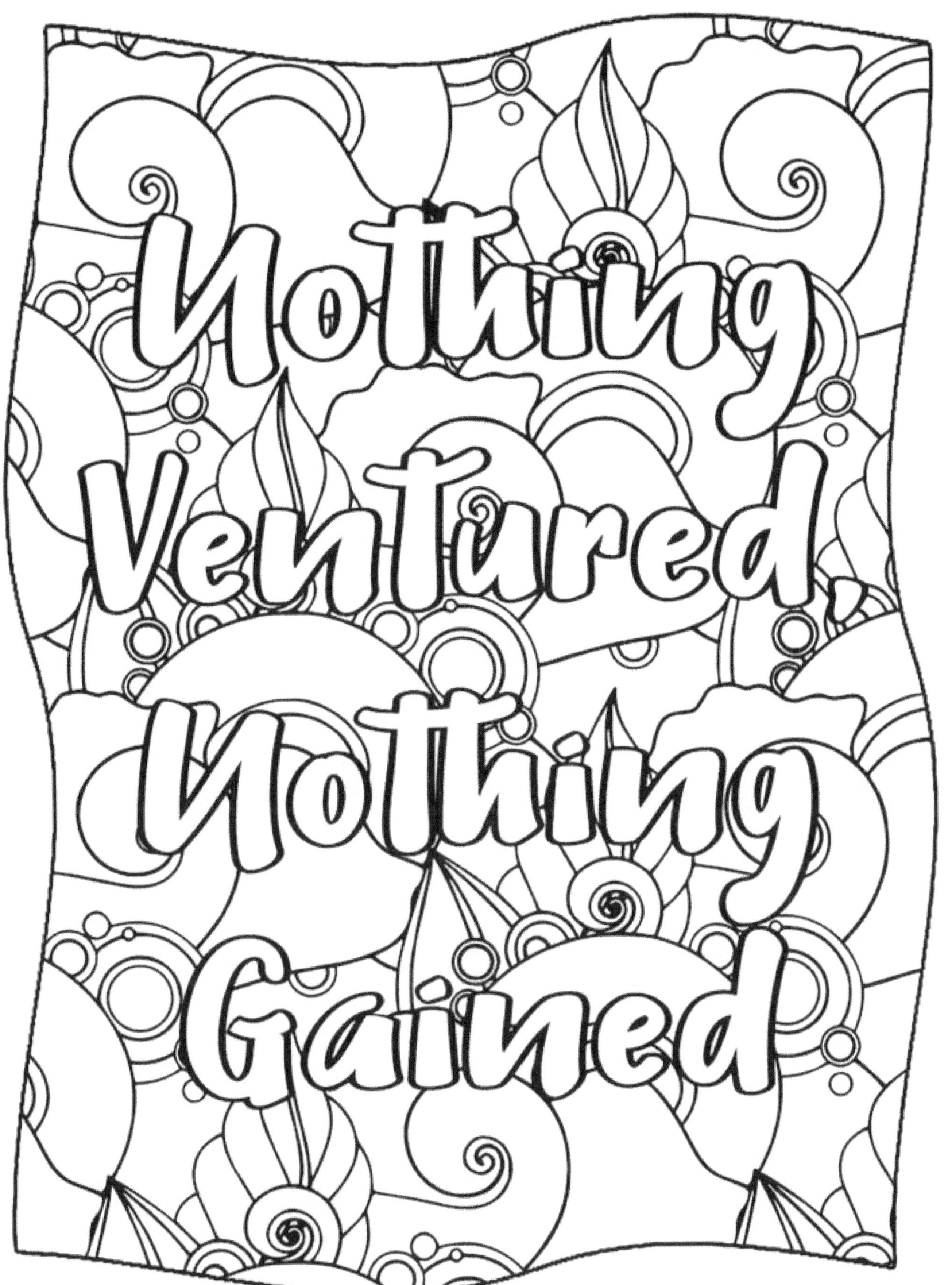

Nothing
Ventured
Nothing
Gained

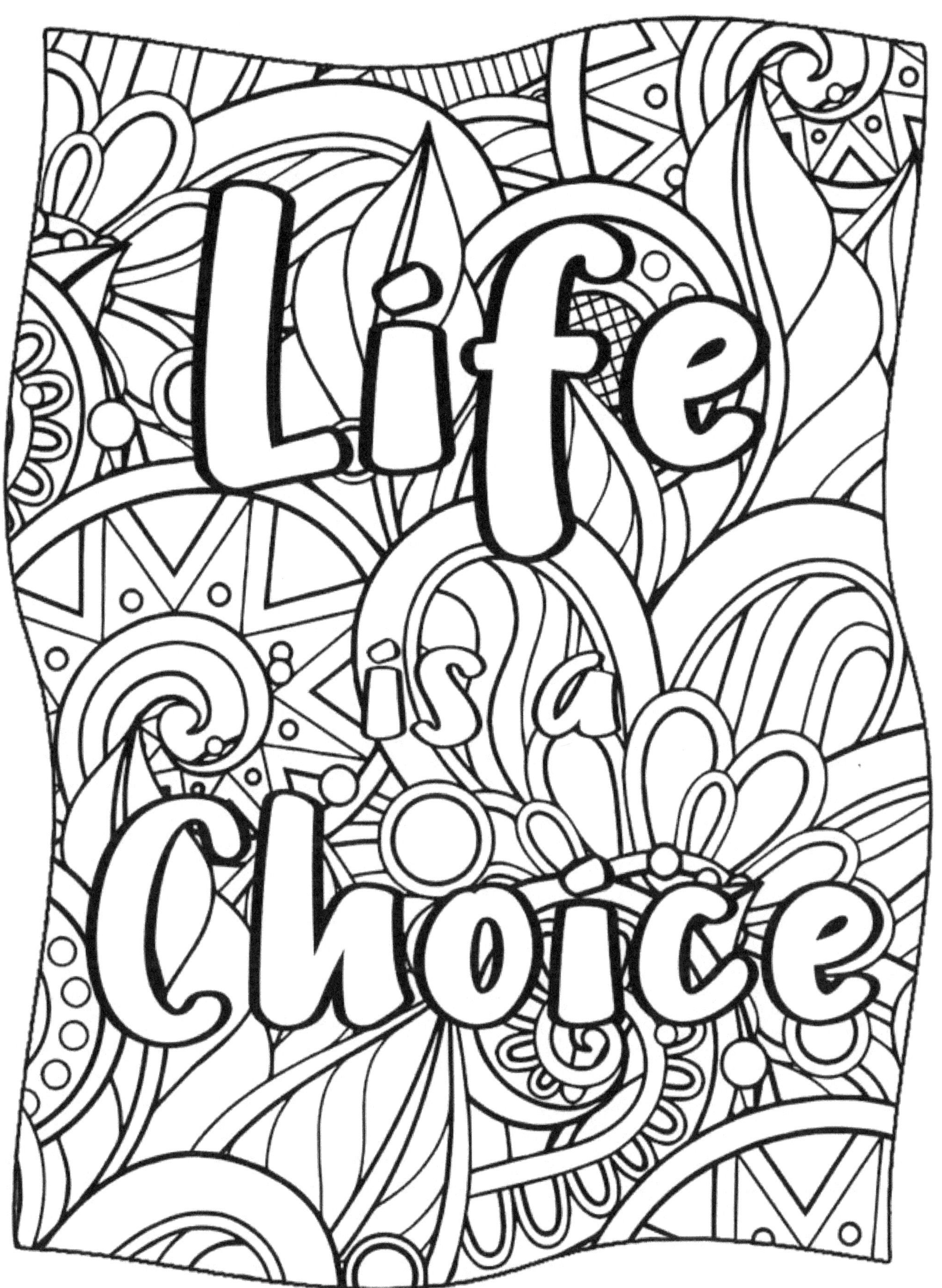

Life
is a
Choice

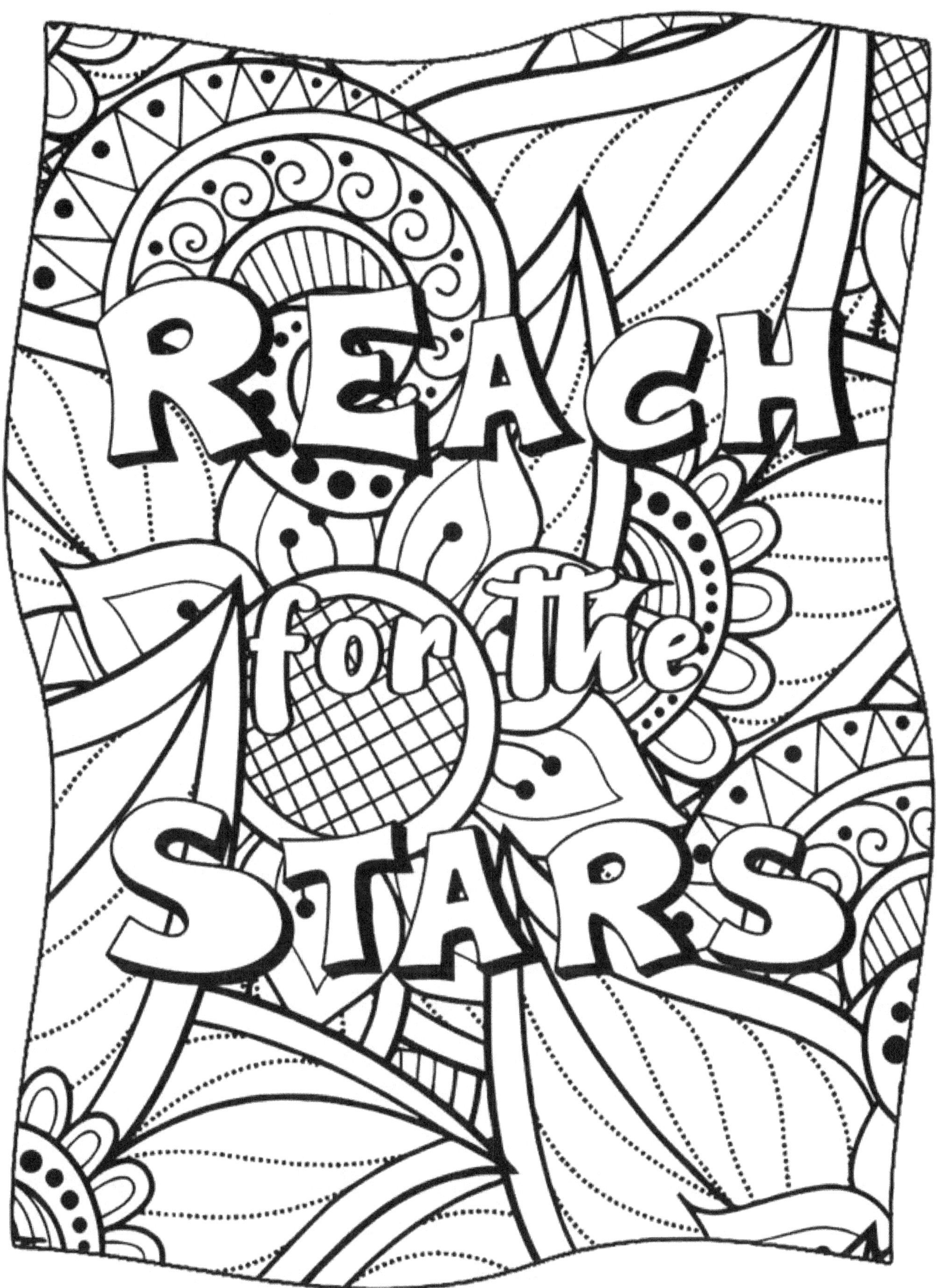

REACH
for the
STARS

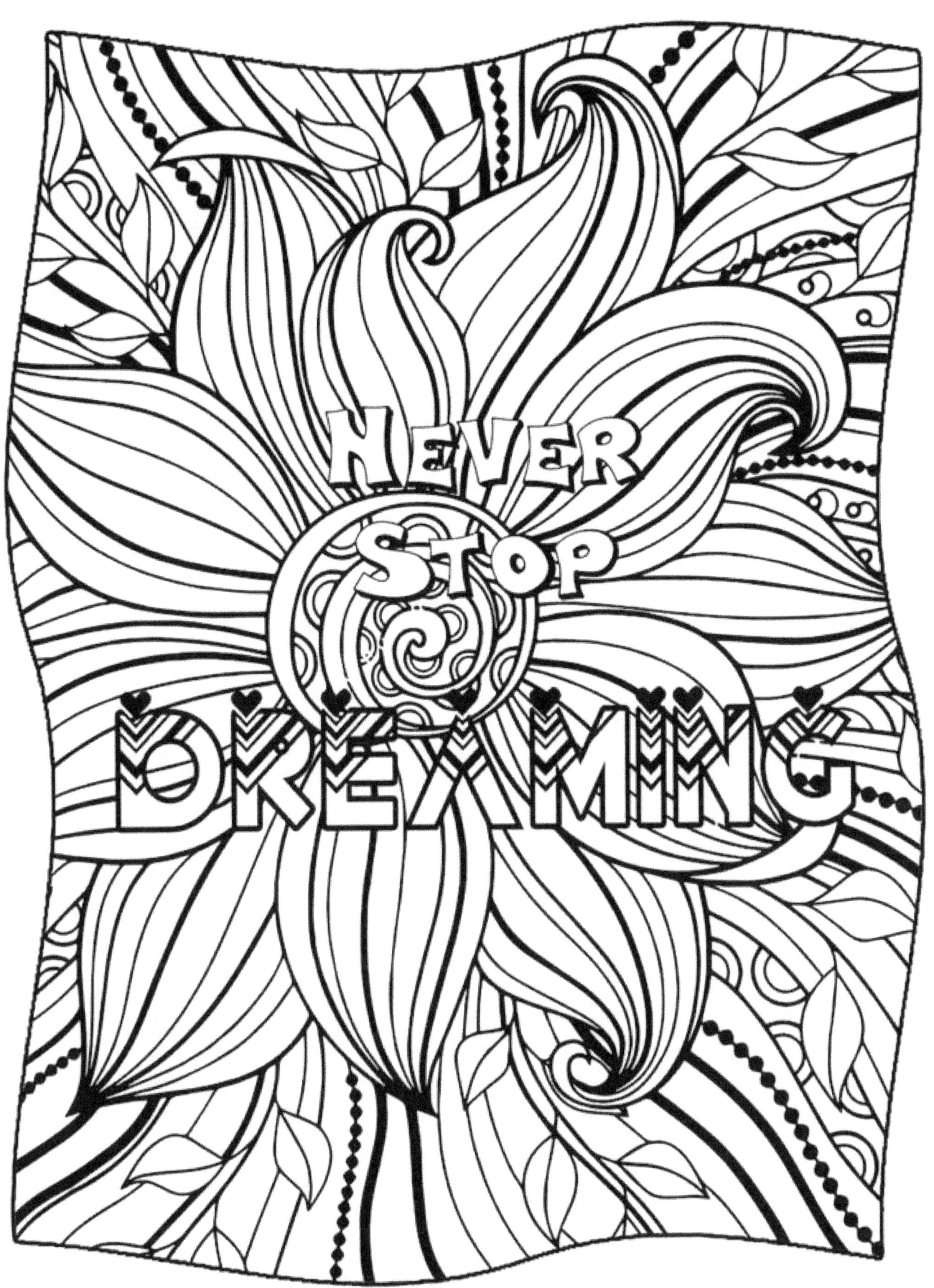

NEVER
STOP
DREAMING

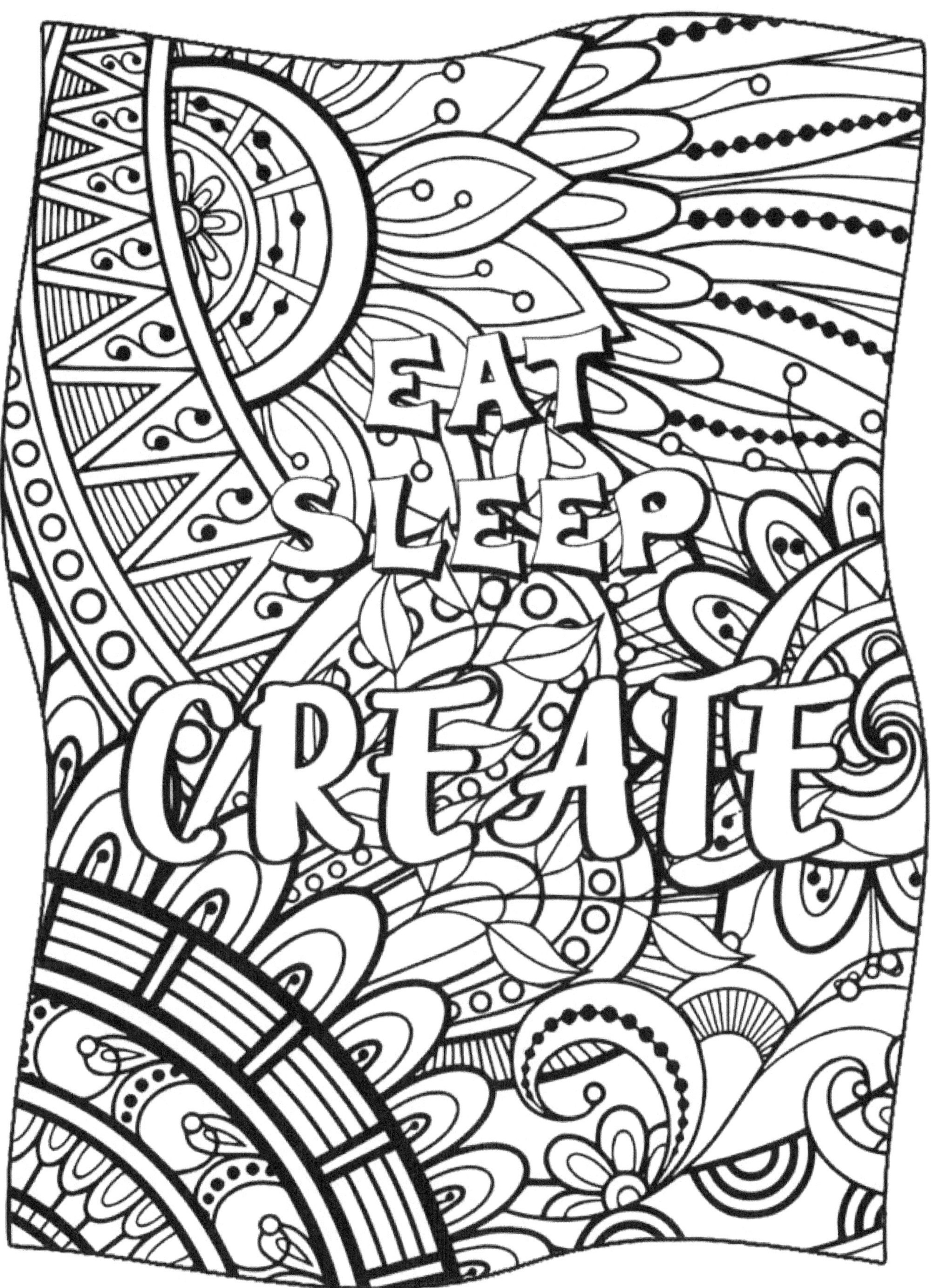

EAT
SLEEP
CREATE

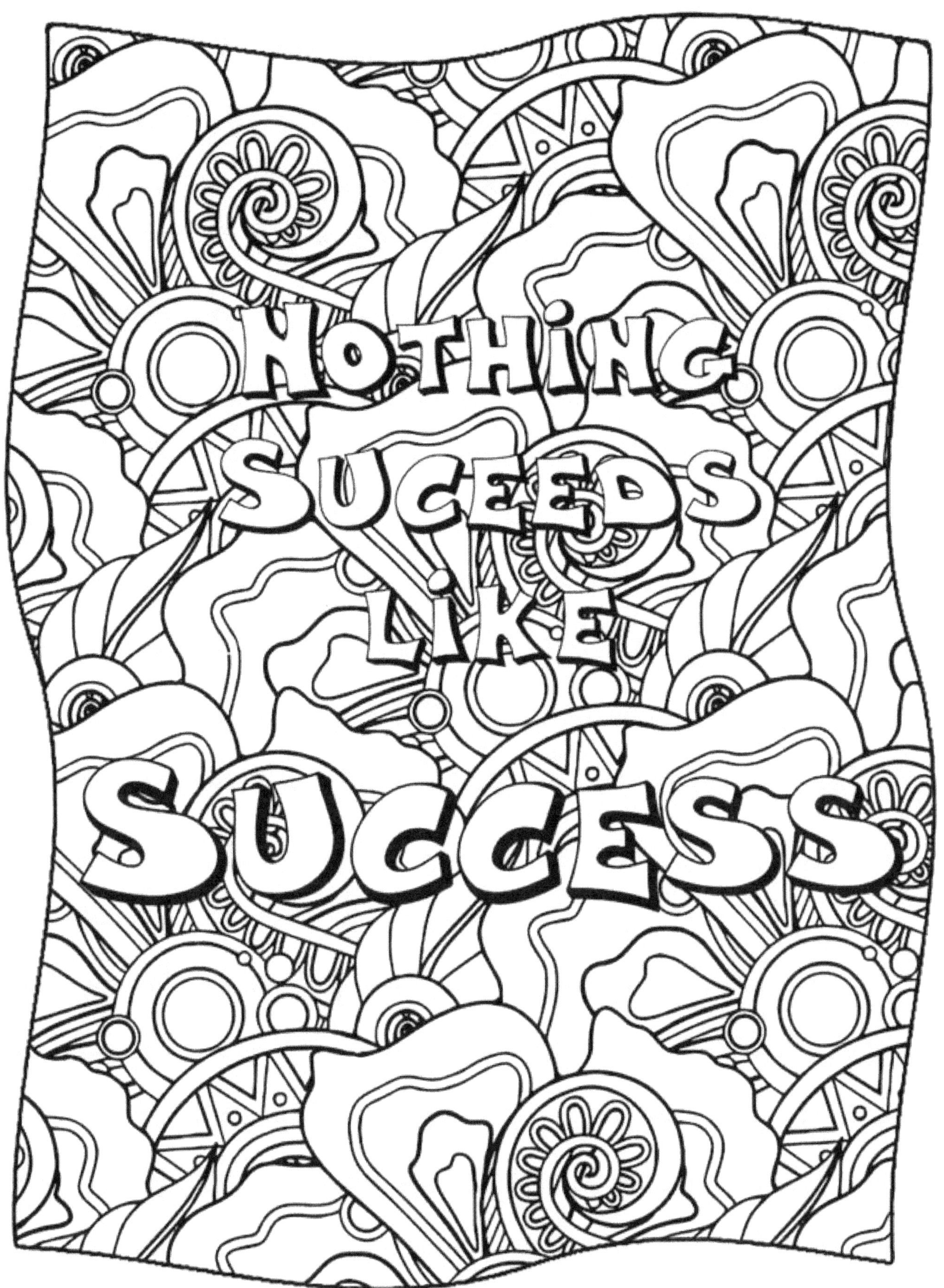

NOTHING
SUCEEDS
LIKE
SUCCESS

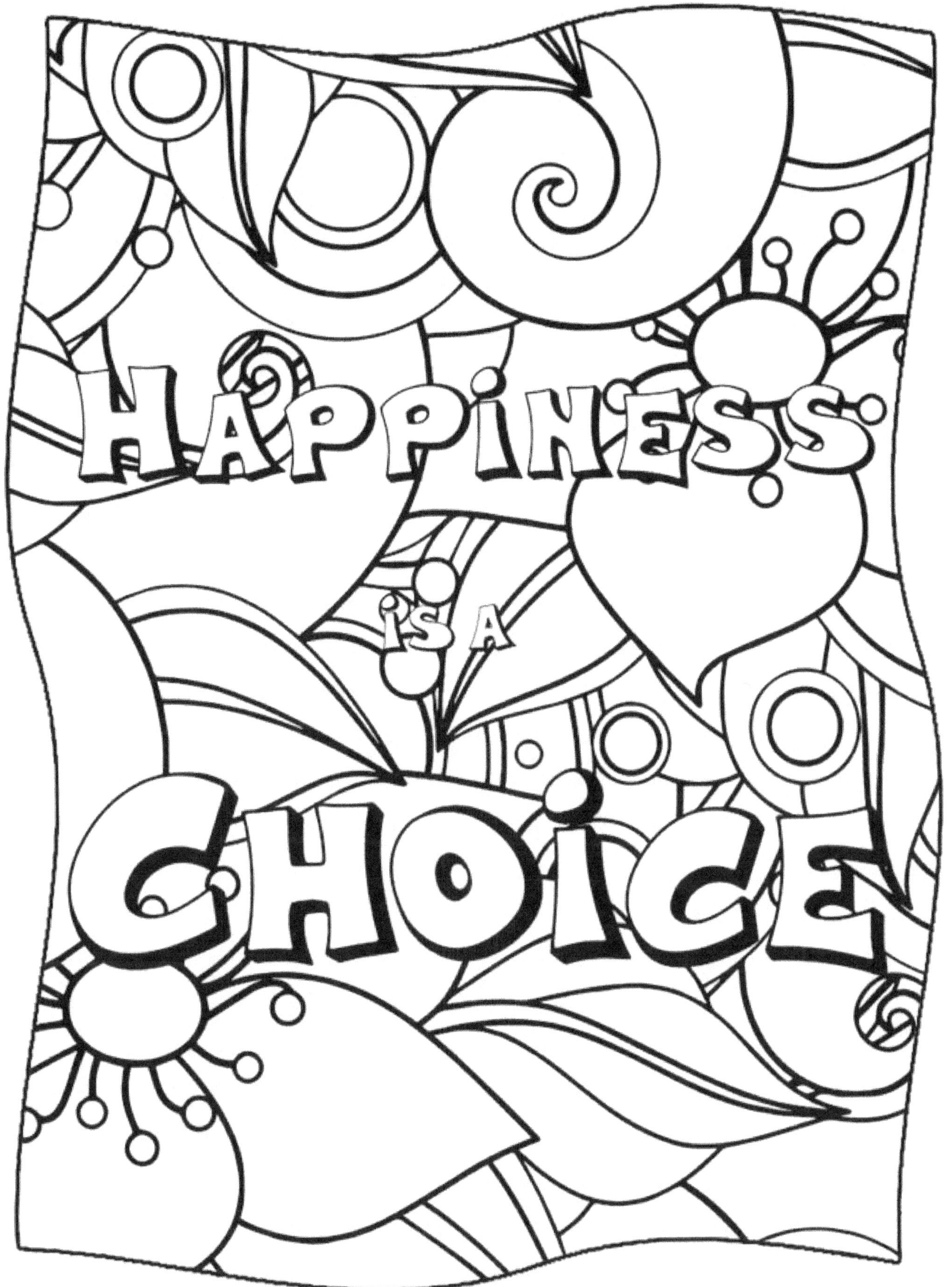

HAPPINESS
IS A
CHOICE

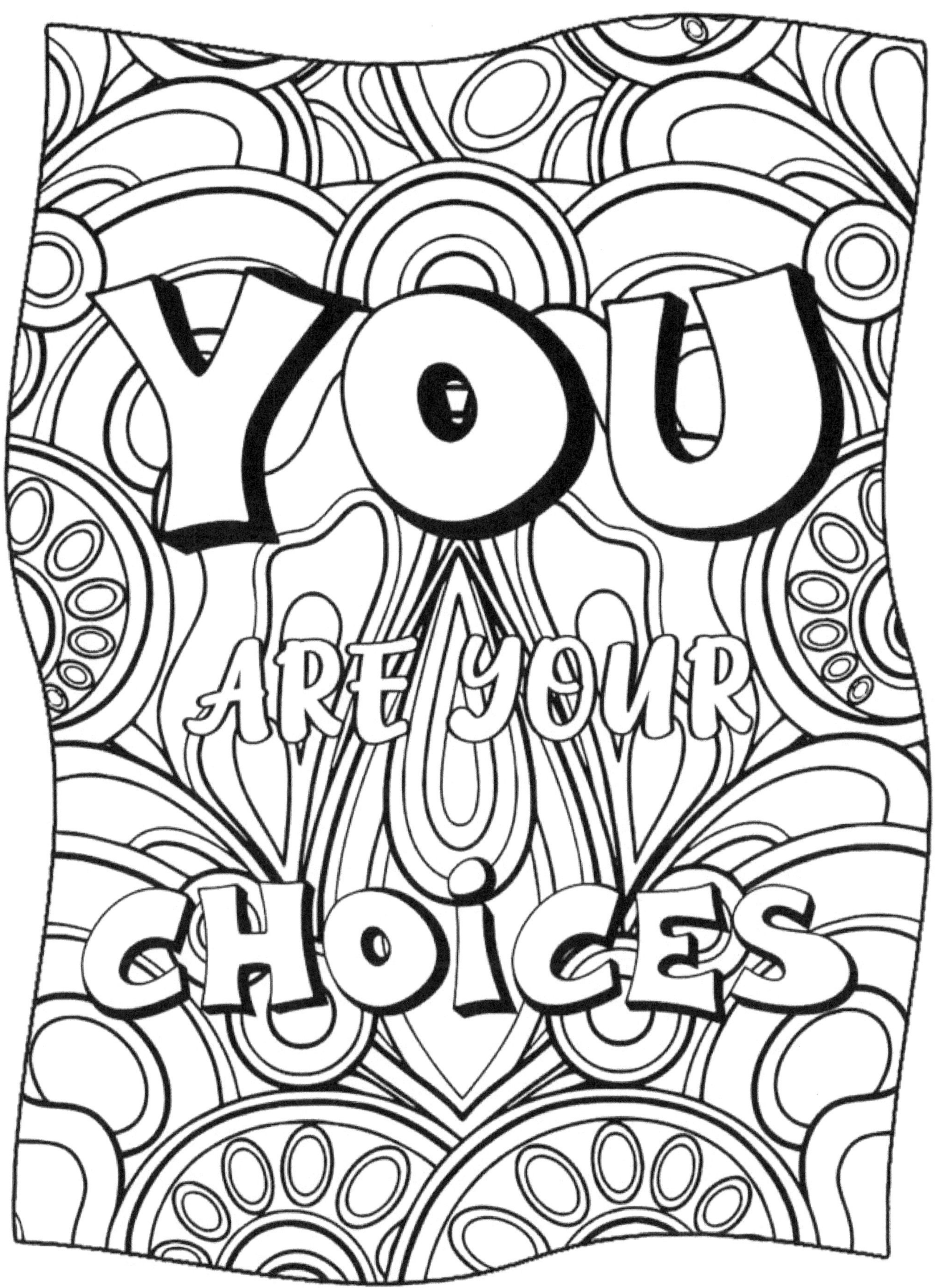

YOU
ARE YOUR
CHOICES

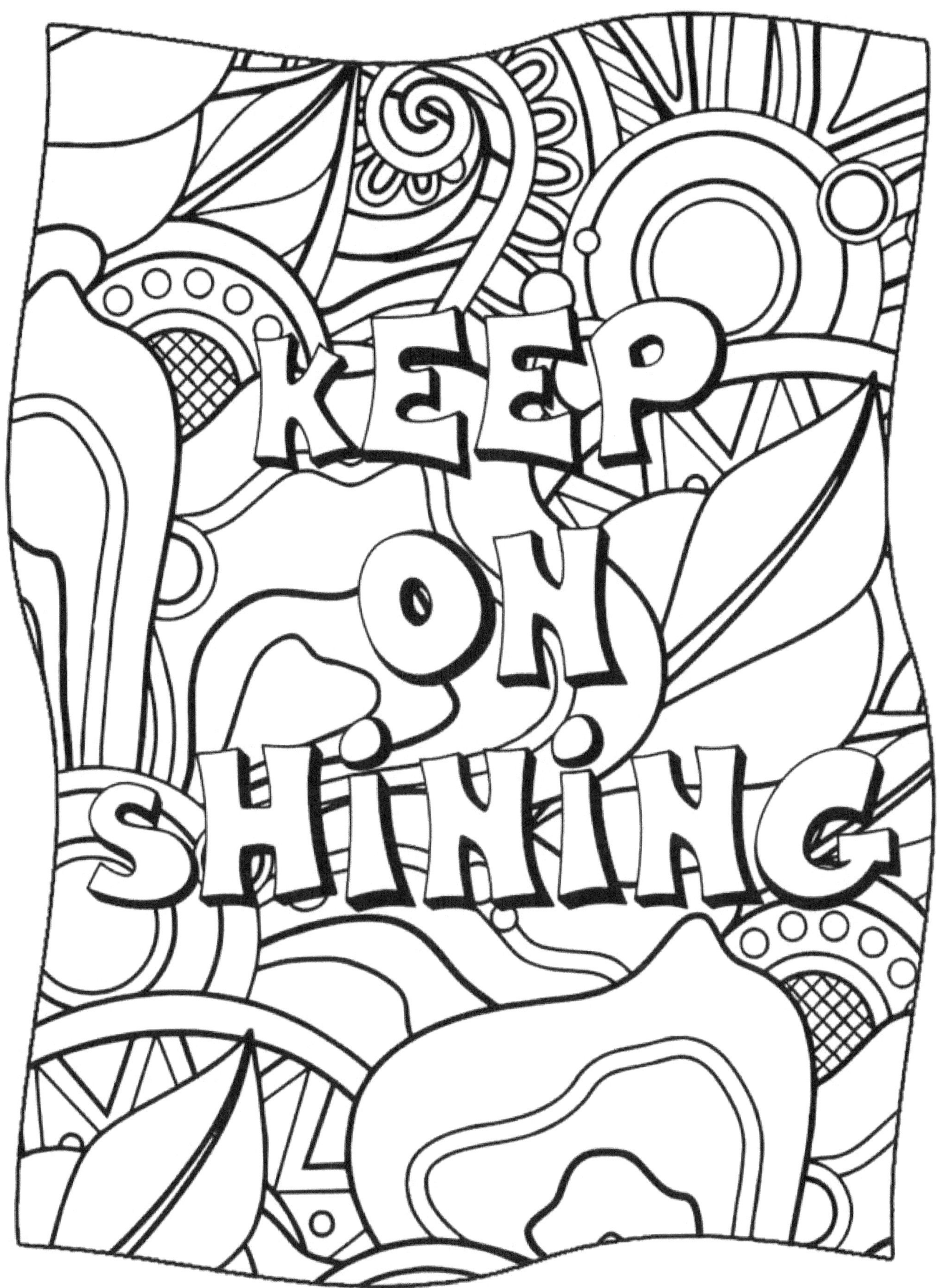

KEEP
ON
SHINING

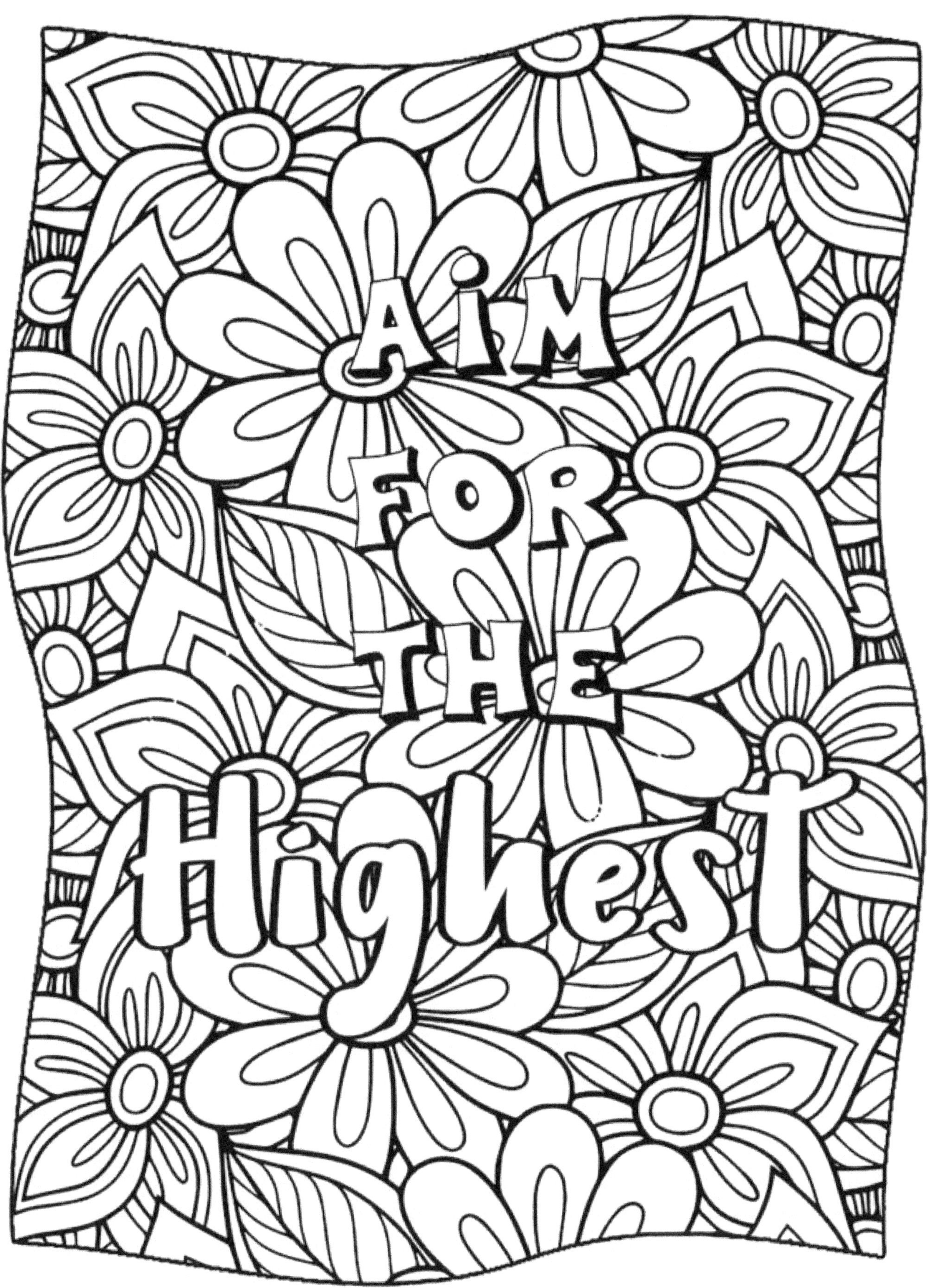

Aim
For
The
Highest

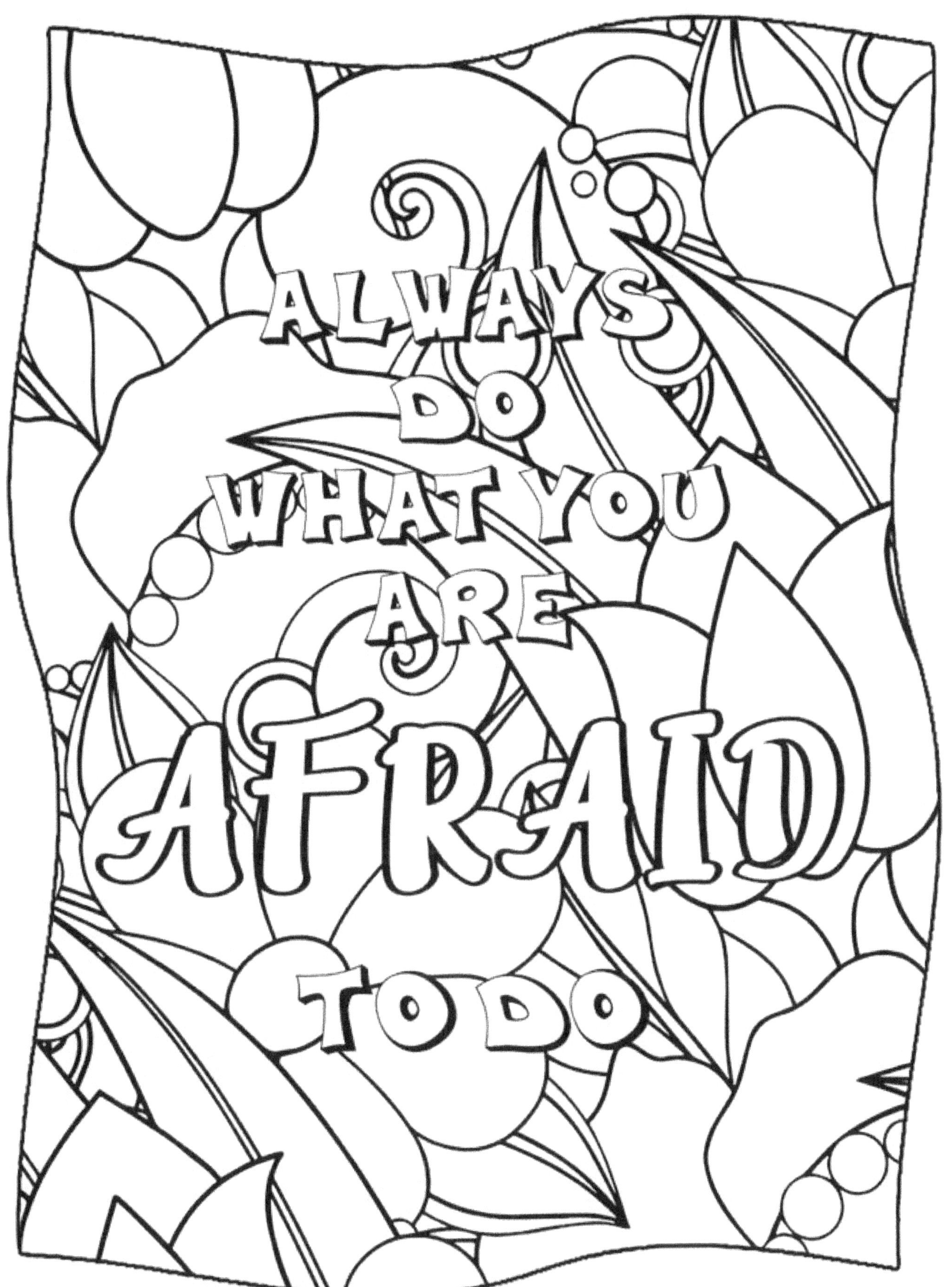

ALWAYS
DO
WHAT YOU
ARE
AFRAID
TO DO

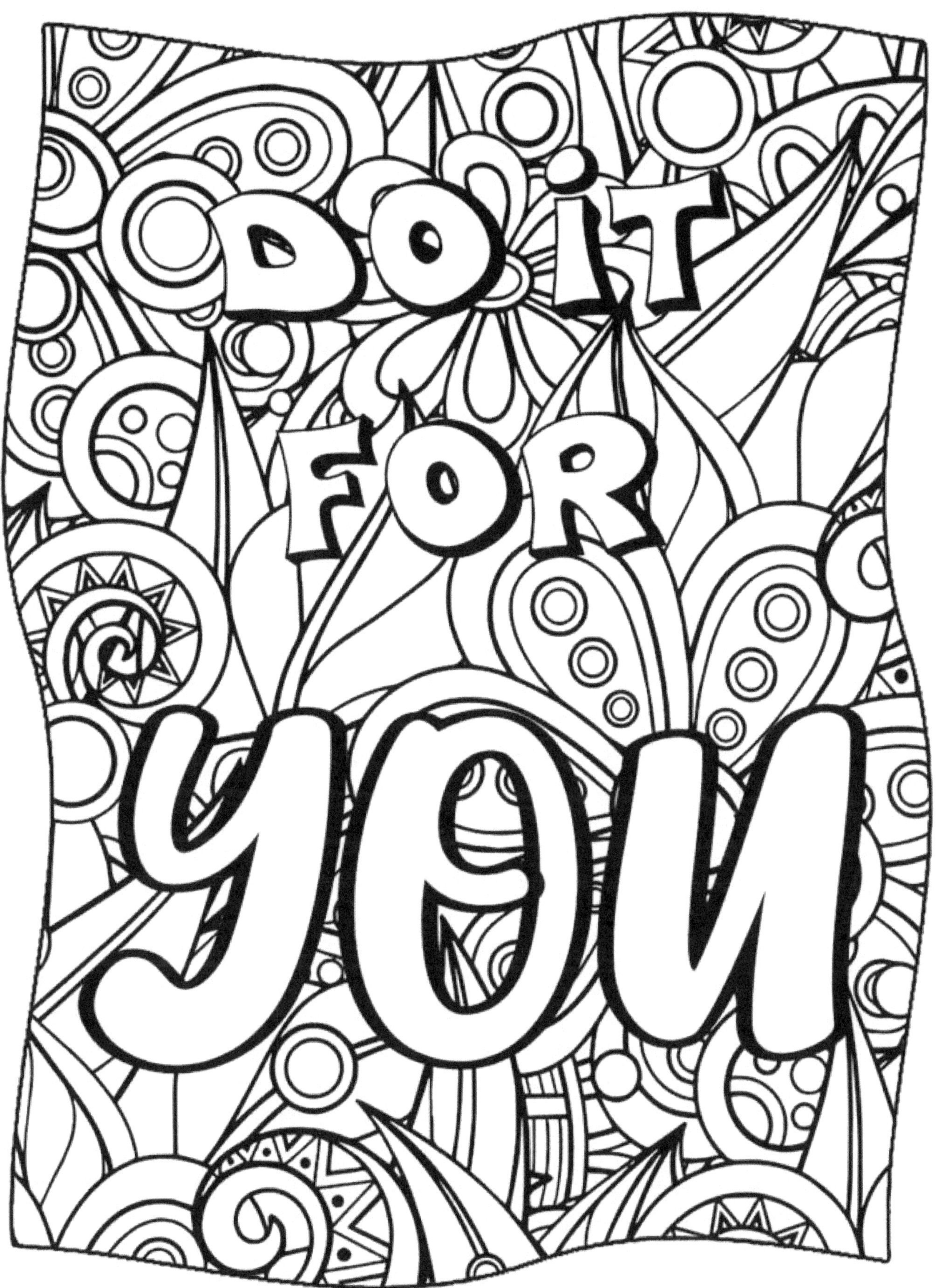

Do it
for
You

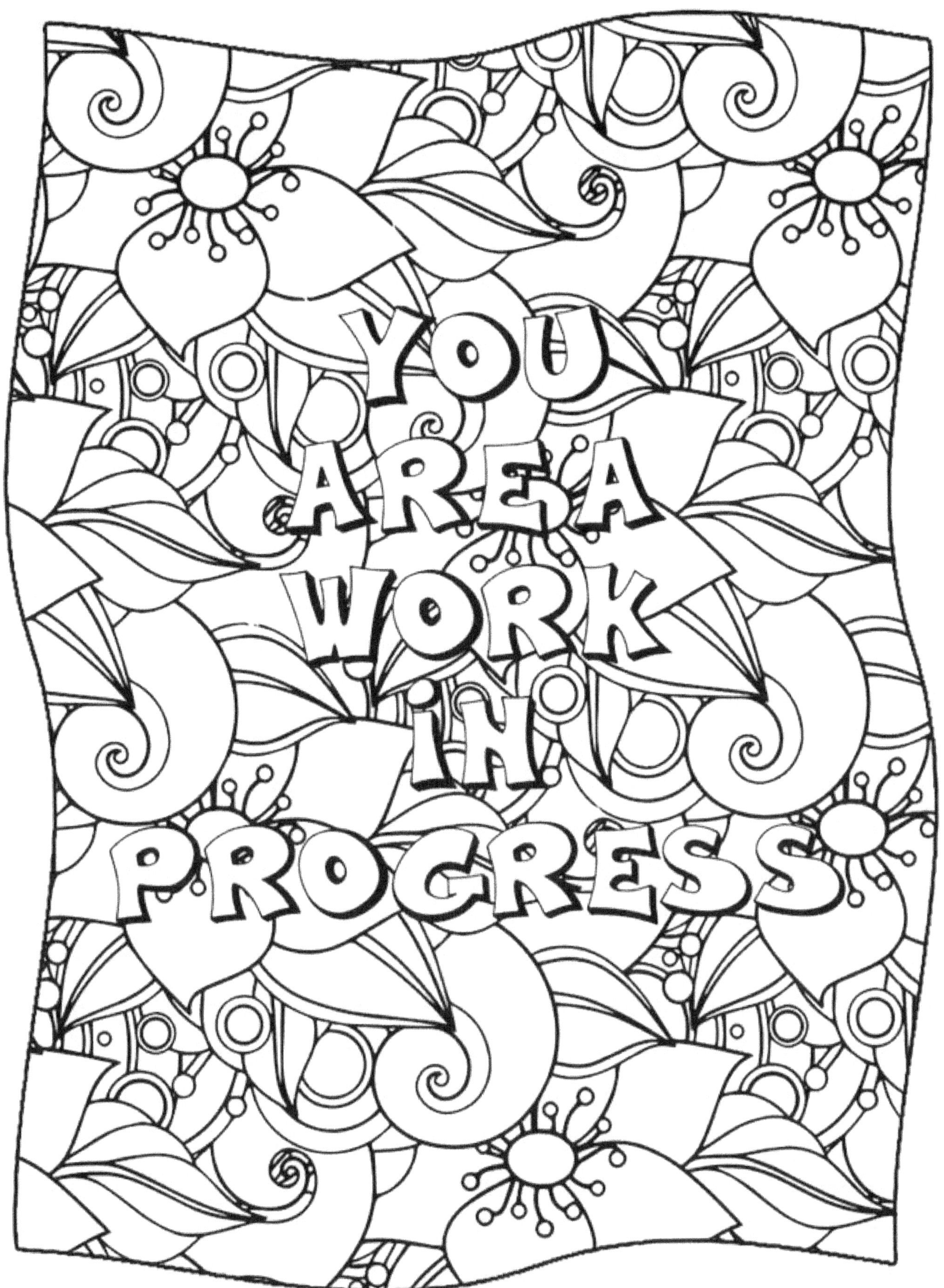

YOU
ARE A
WORK
IN
PROGRESS

CREATE
YOUR
OWN
Sunshine

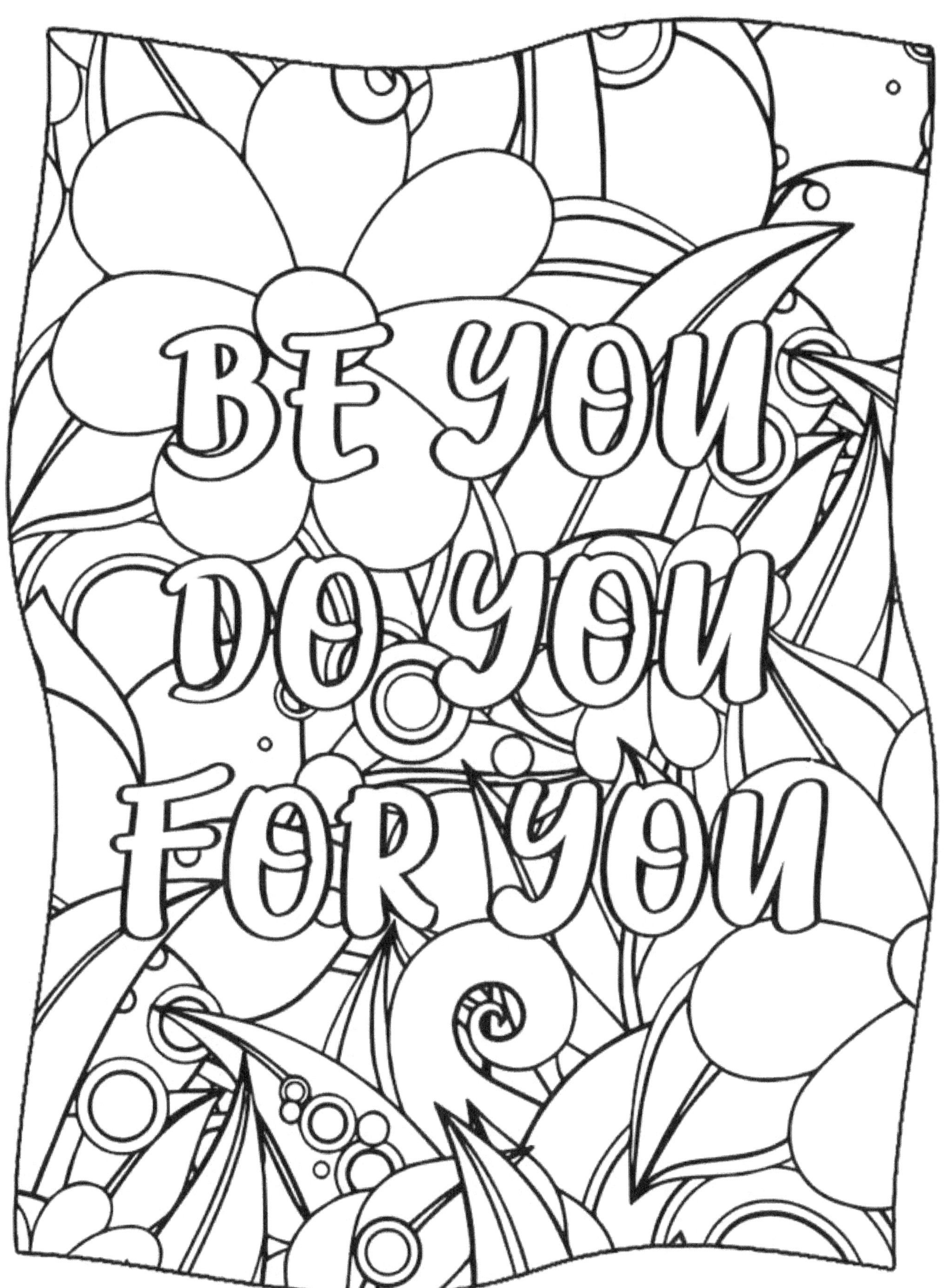

BE YOU
DO YOU
FOR YOU

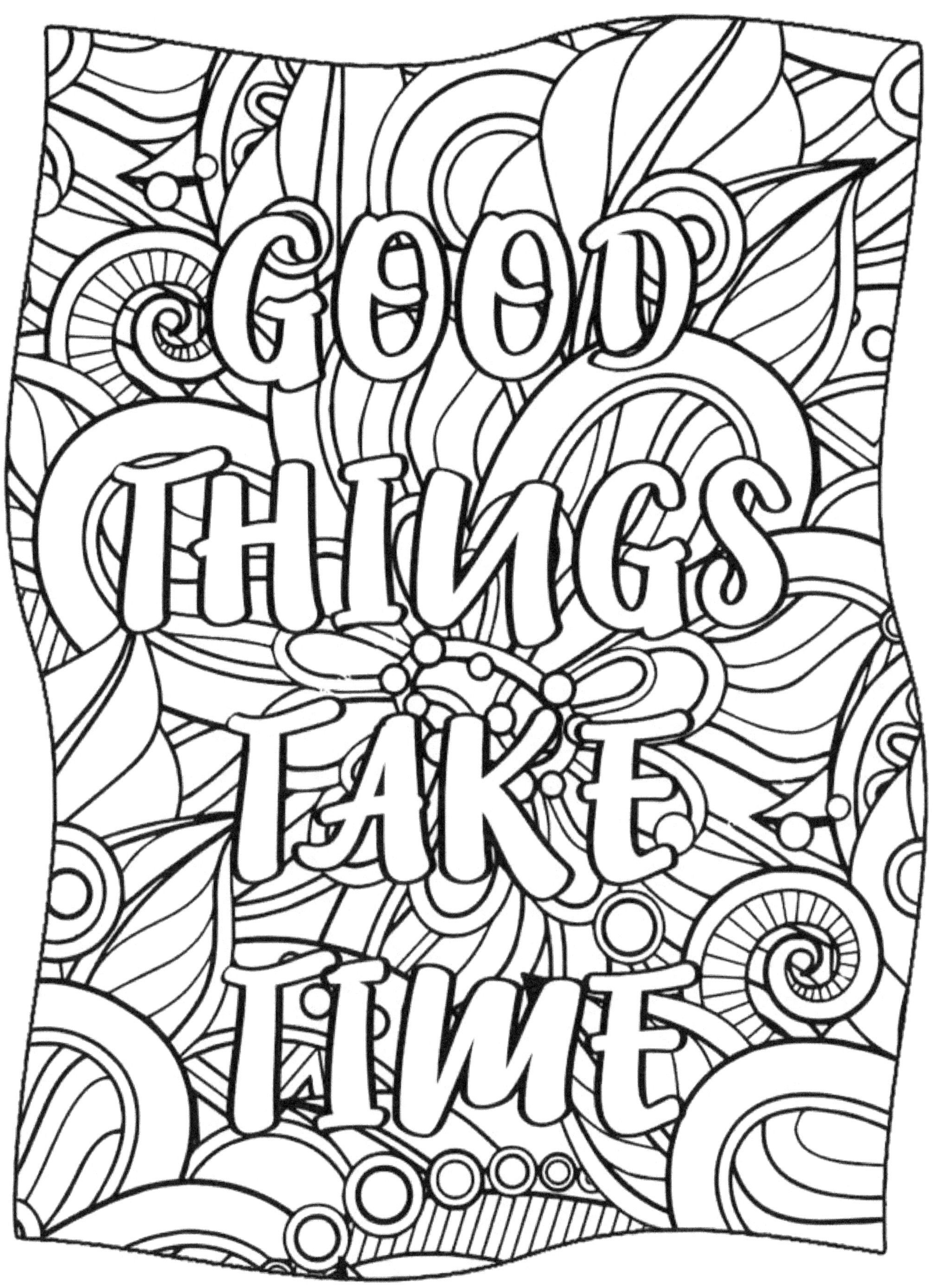

GOOD
THINGS
TAKE
TIME

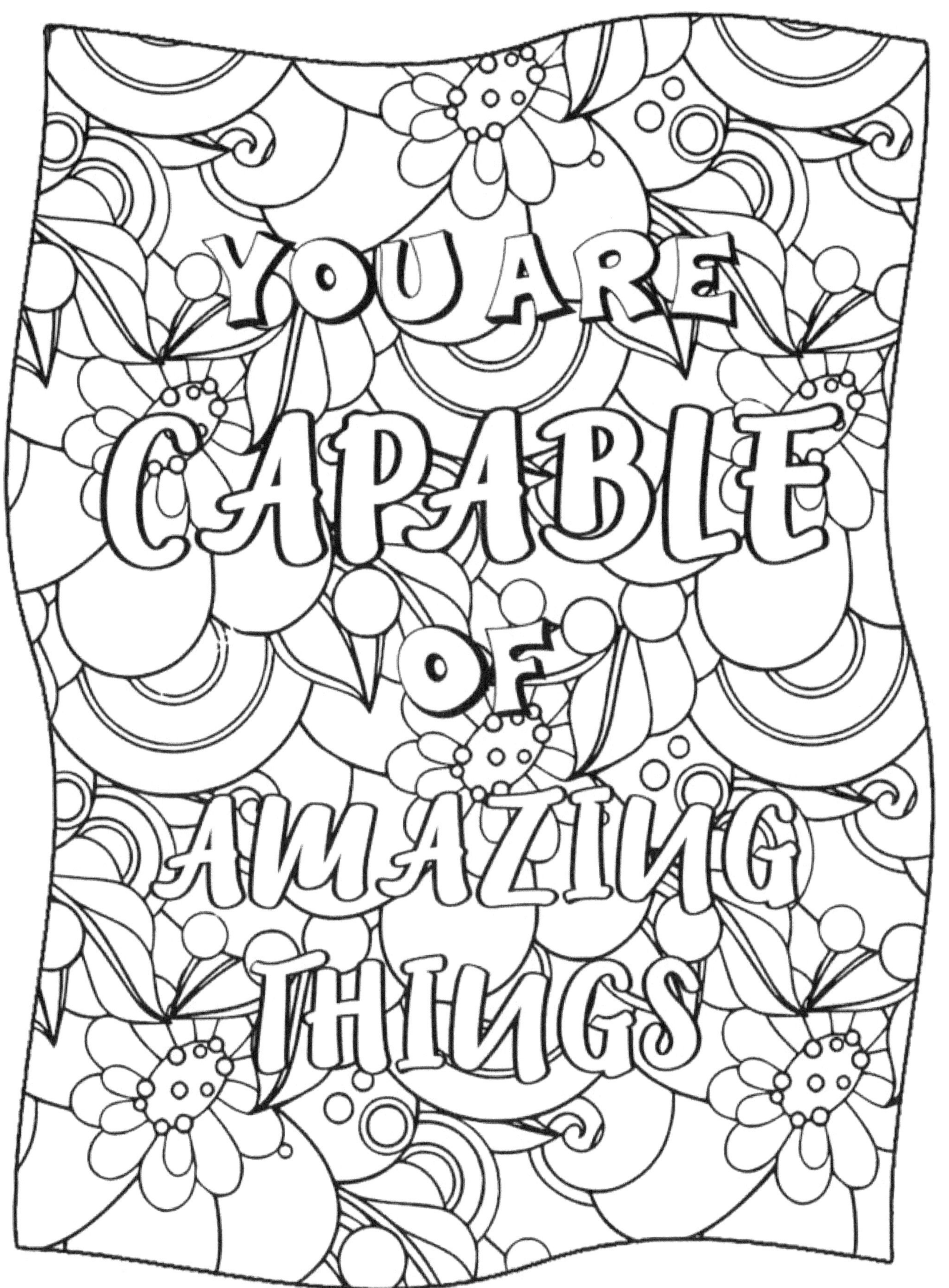

YOU ARE
CAPABLE
OF
AMAZING
THINGS

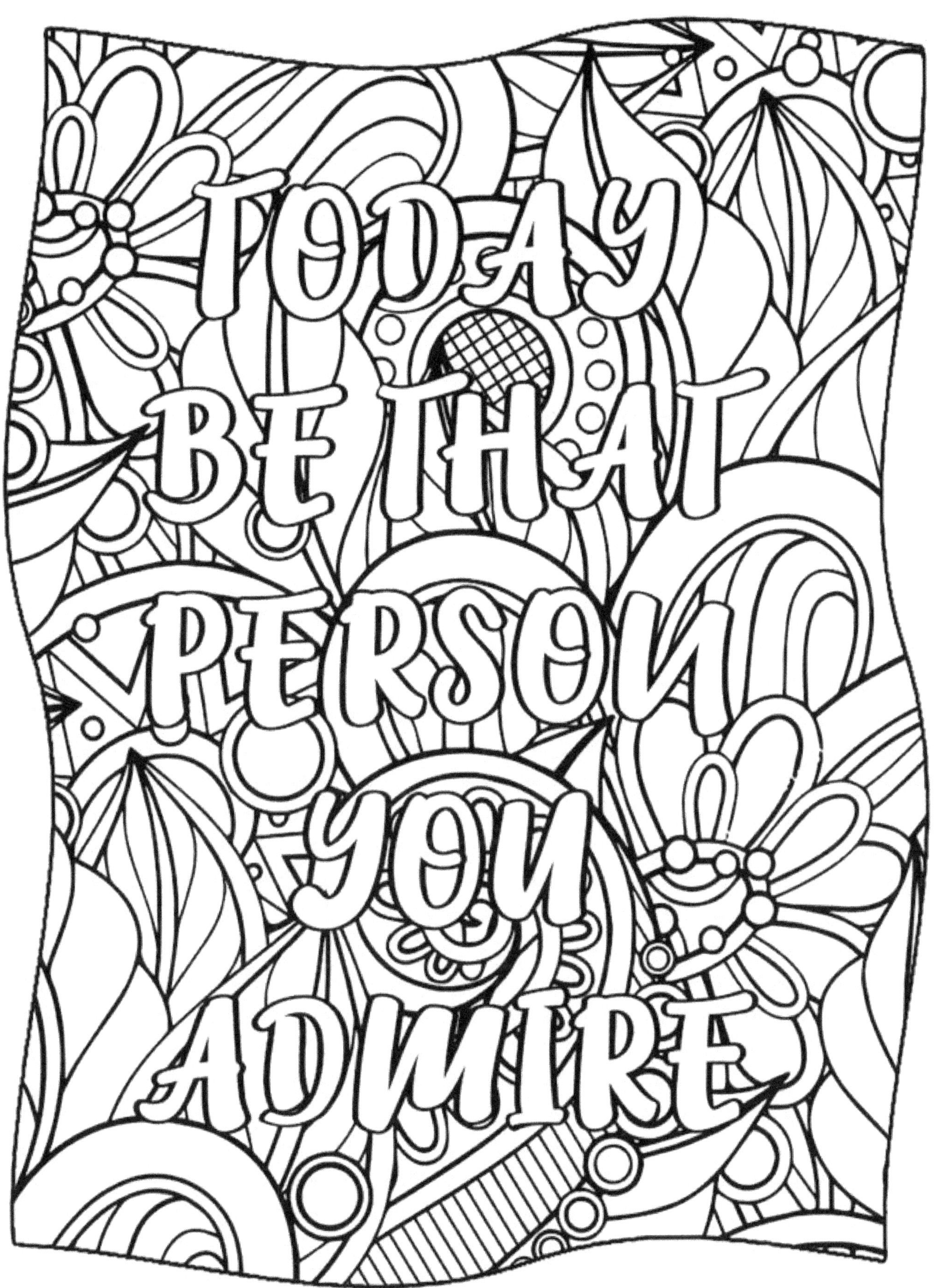

TODAY
BE THAT
PERSON
YOU
ADMIRE

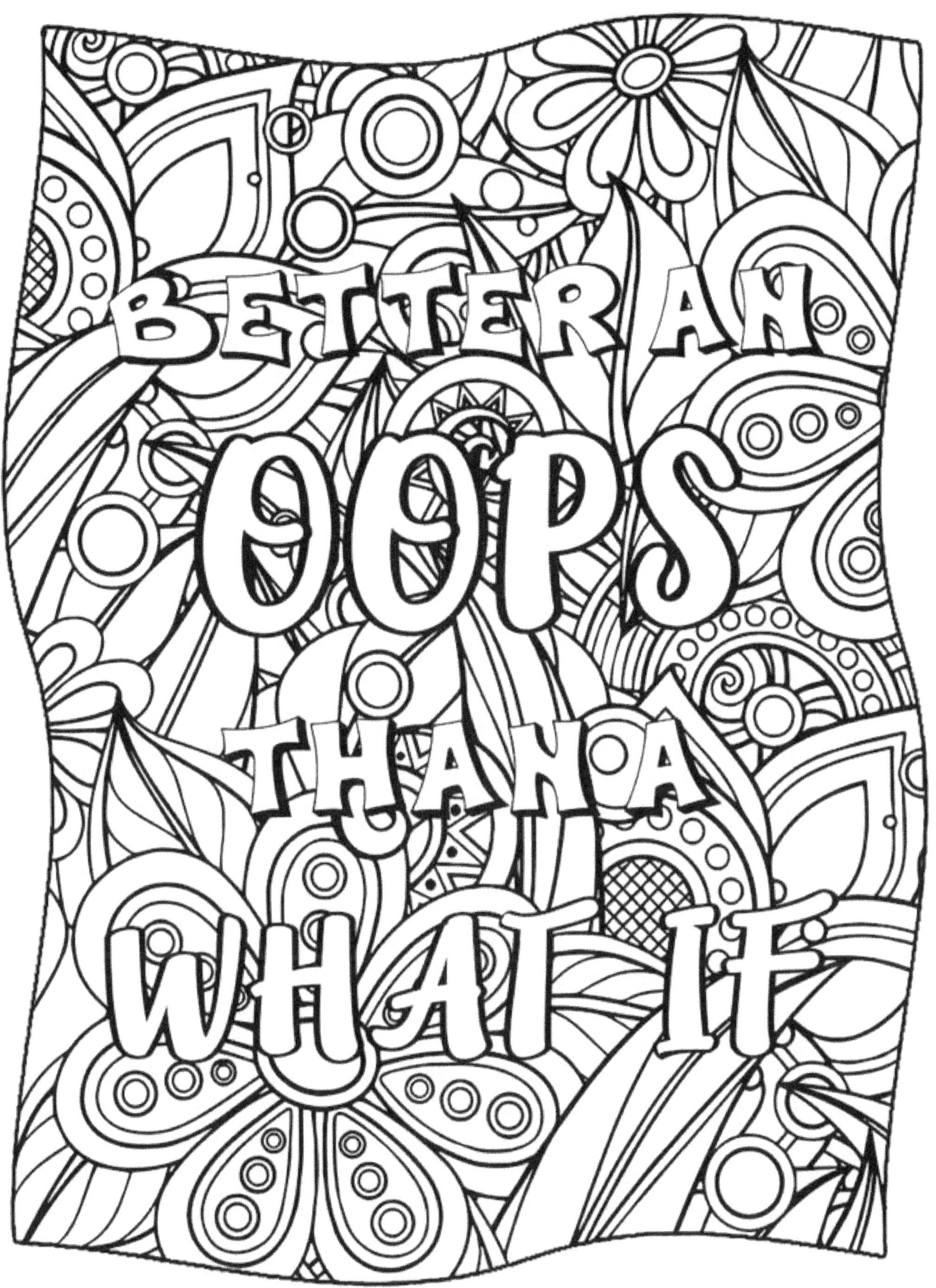

BETTER AN
OOPS
THAN A
WHAT IF

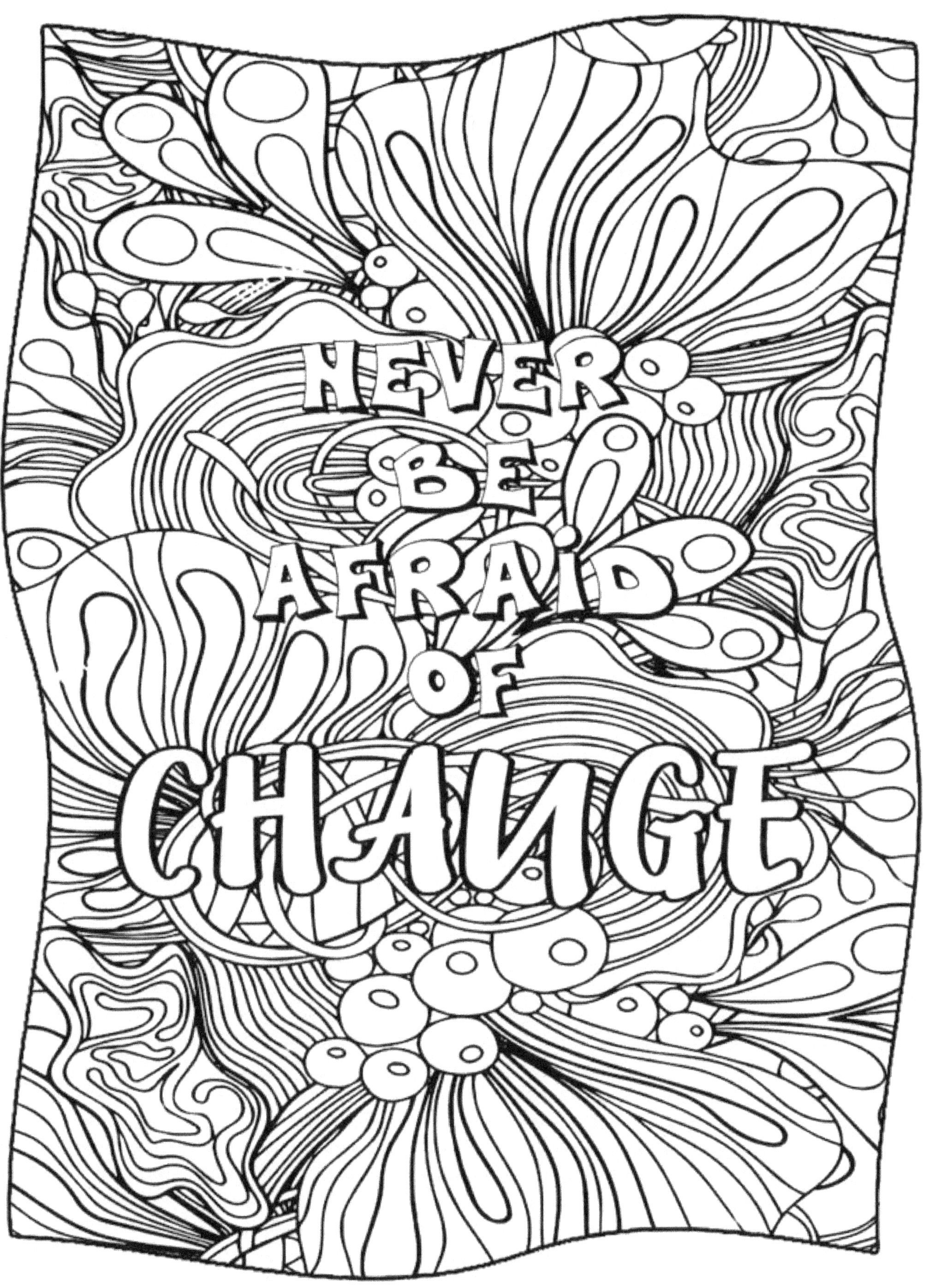

NEVER
BE
AFRAID
OF
CHANGE

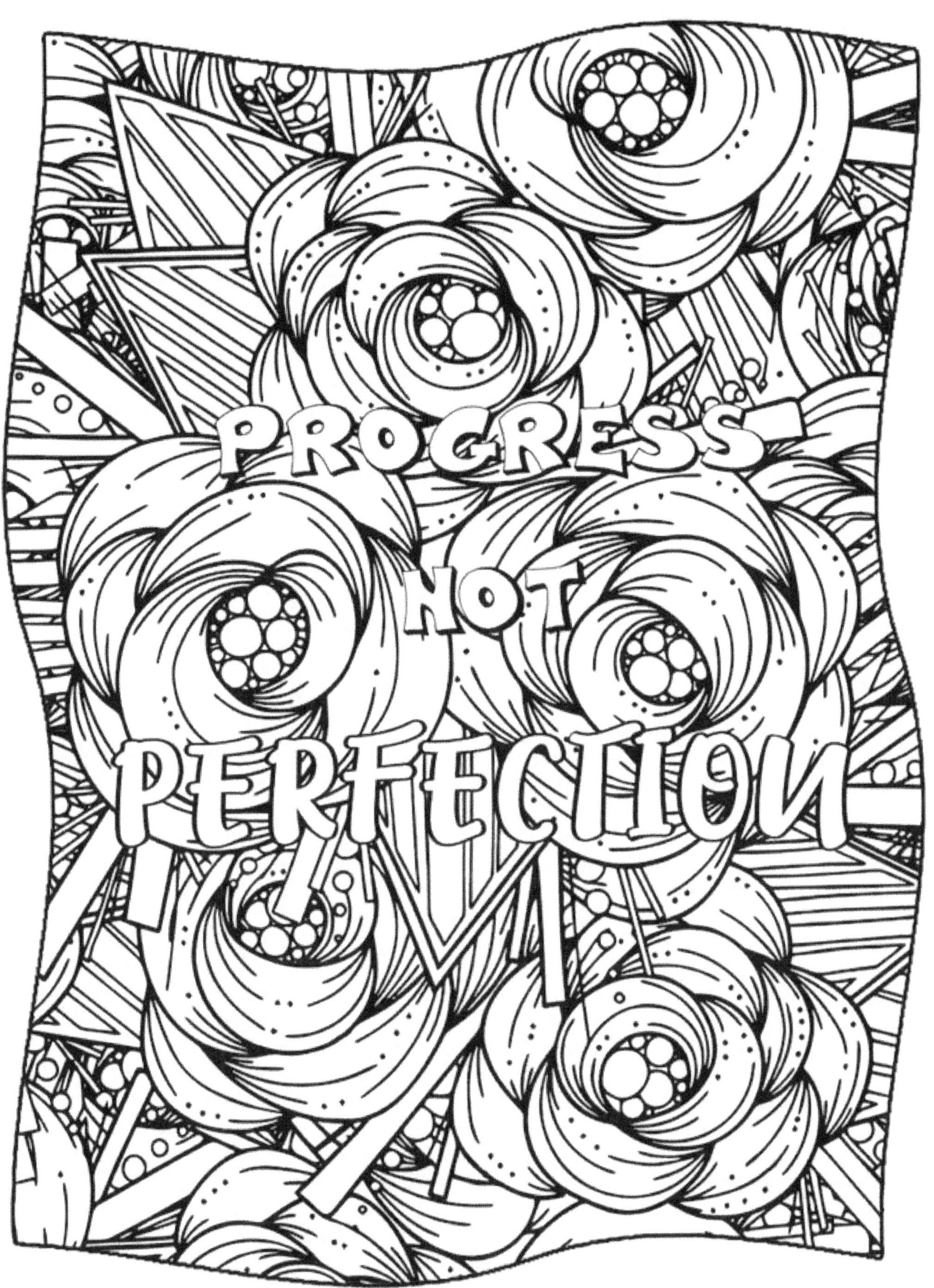
PROGRESS
NOT
PERFECTION

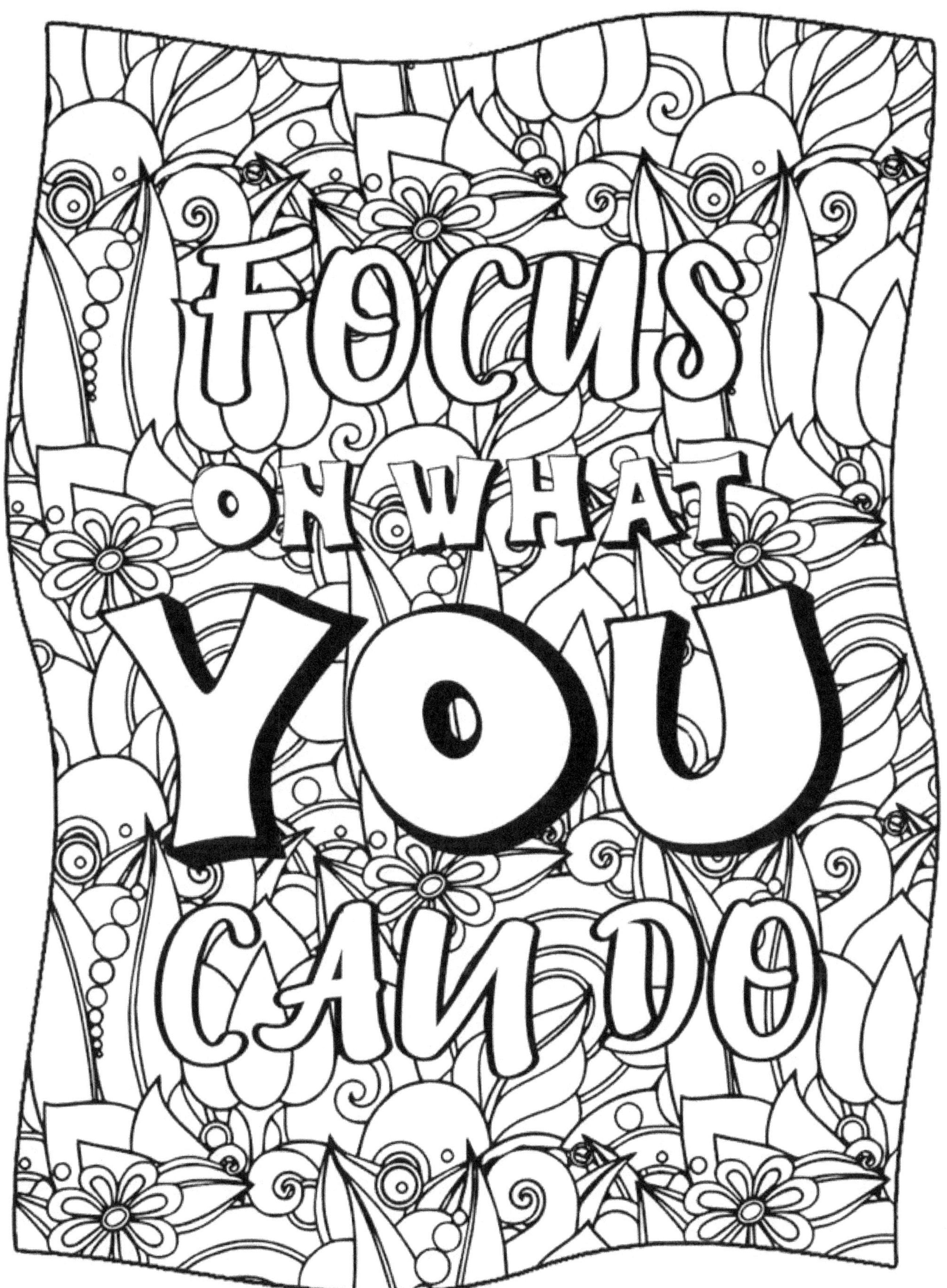

Focus
on what
YOU
can do

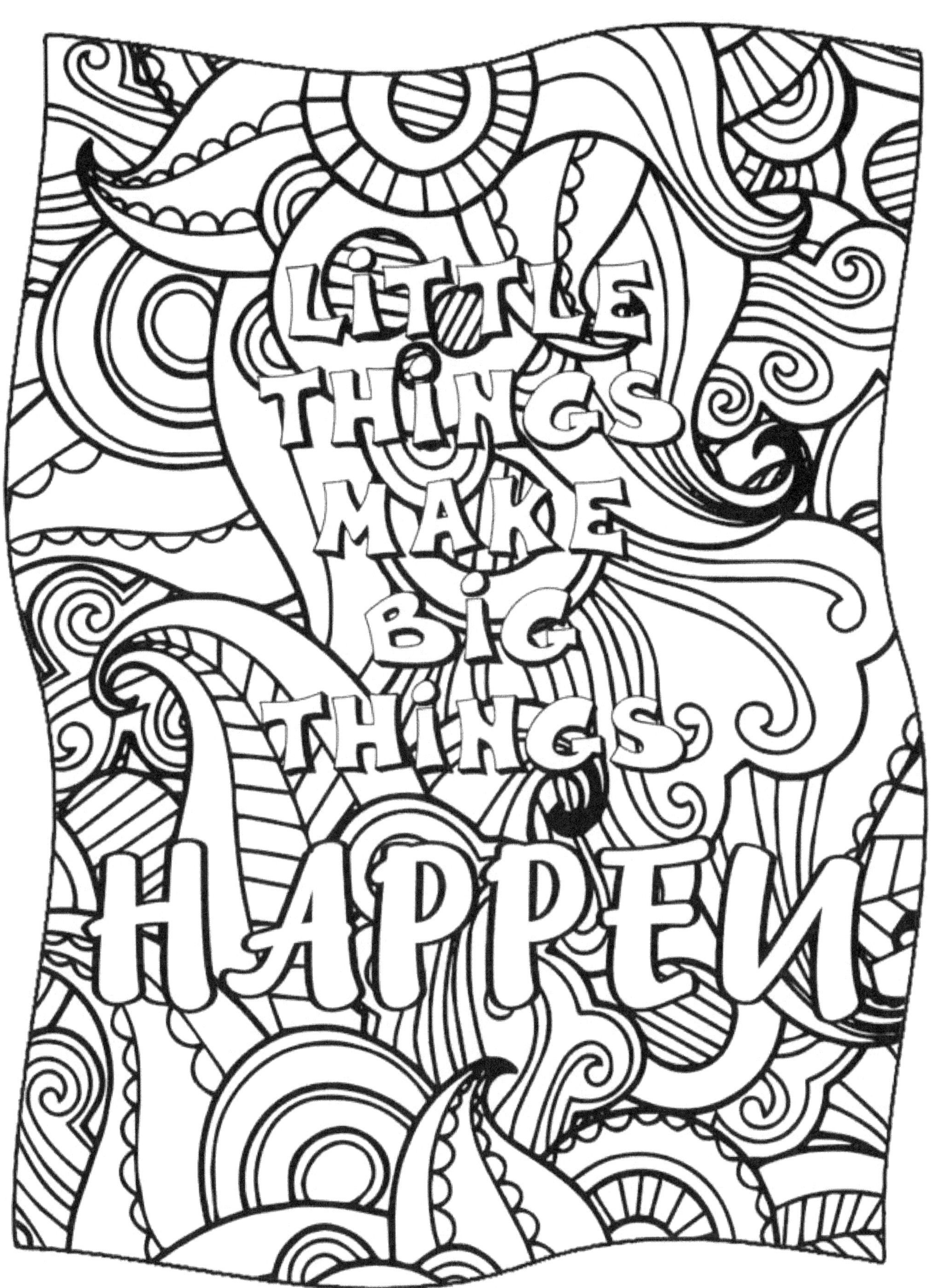

LITTLE
THINGS
MAKE
BIG
THINGS
HAPPEN

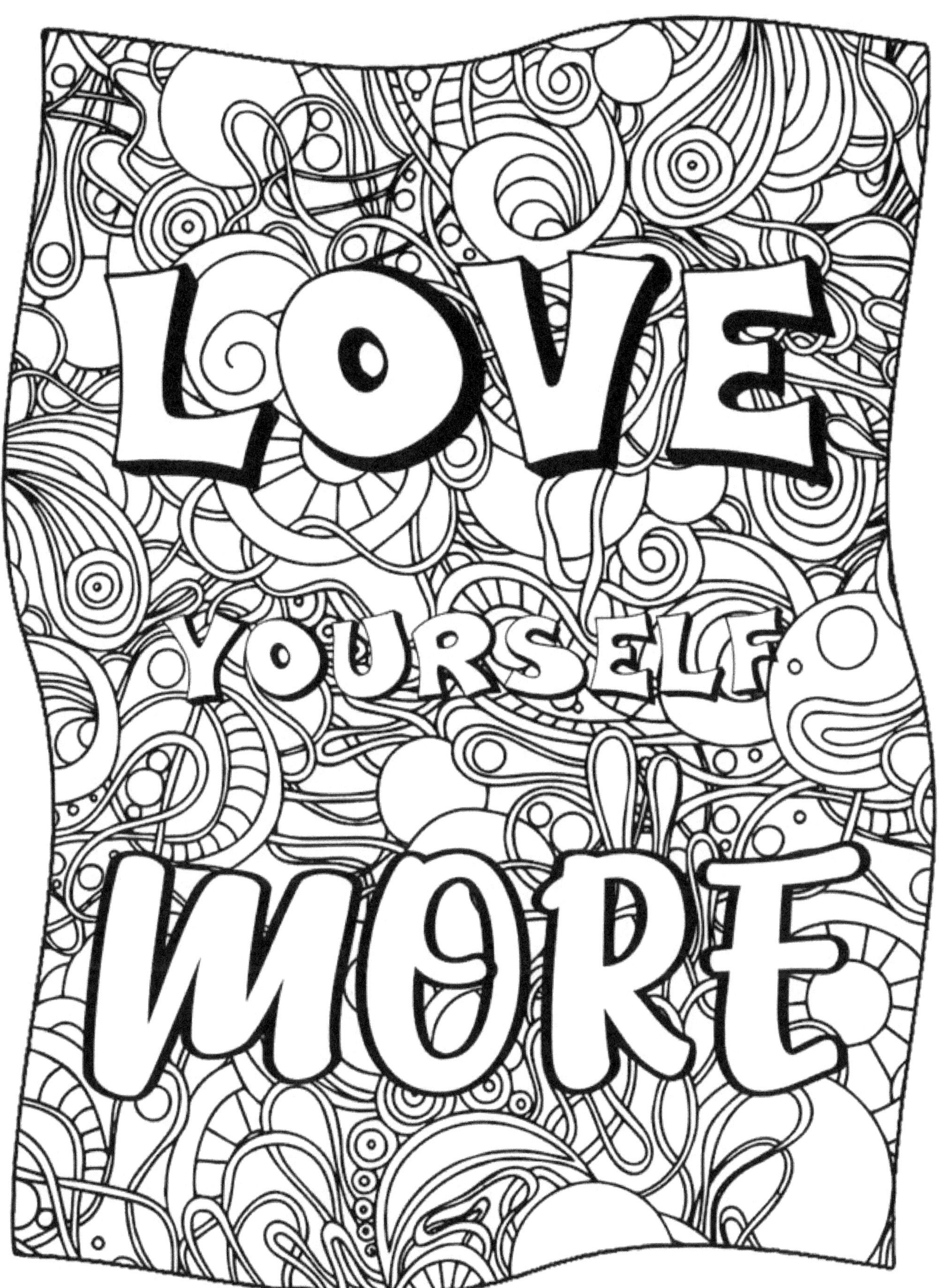

LOVE
YOURSELF
MORE

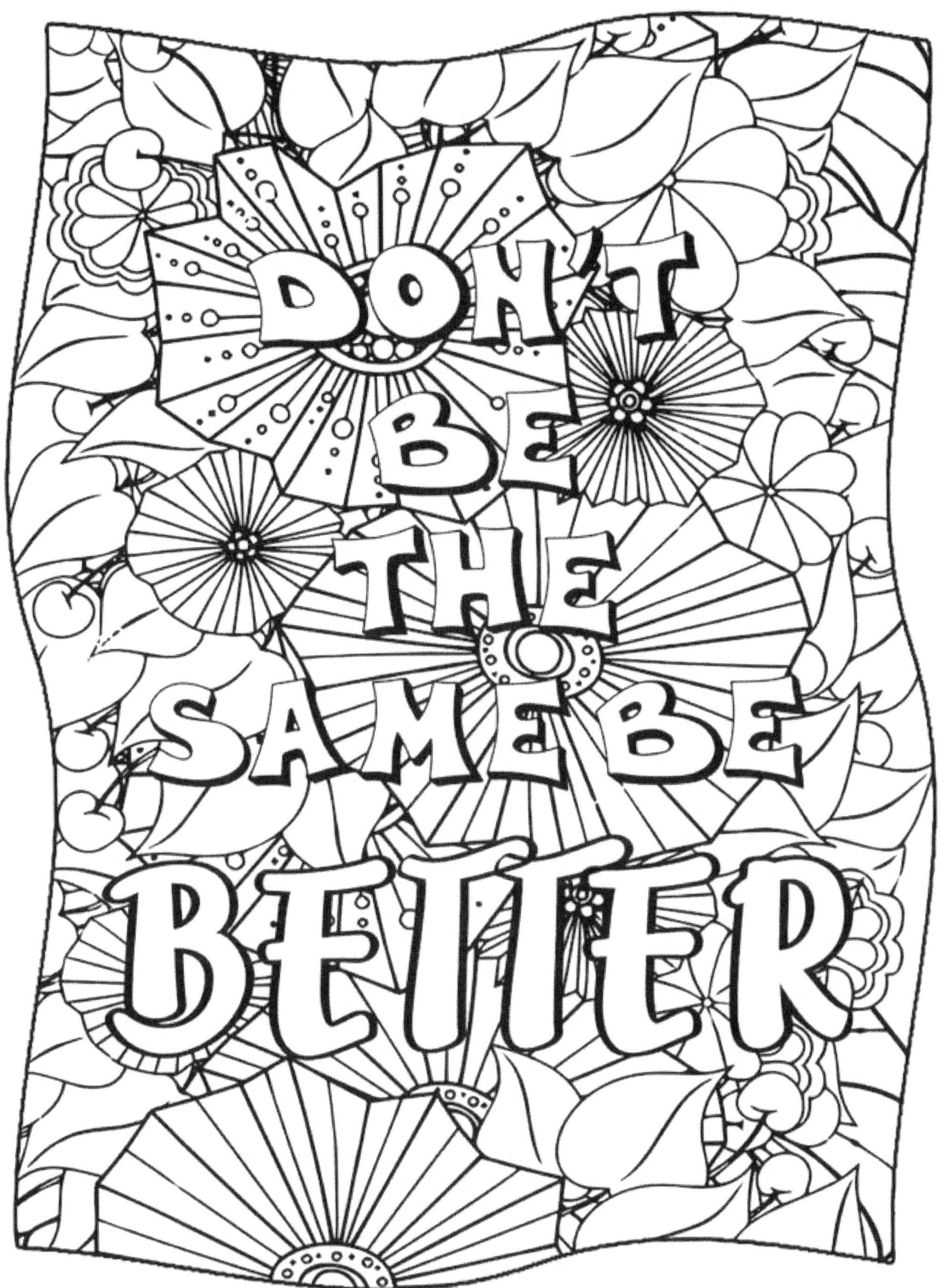

Don't
be
the
same be
Better

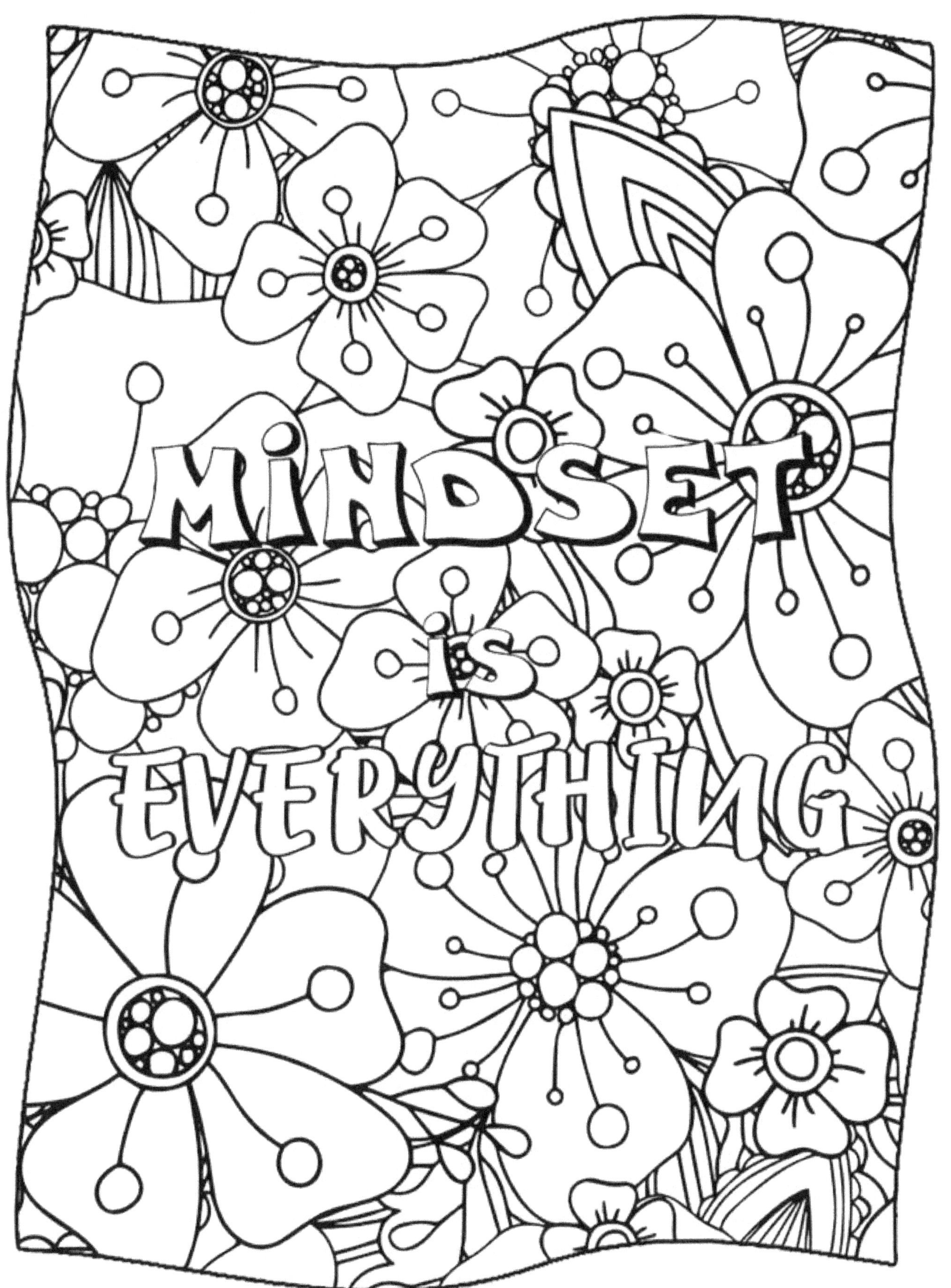

MINDSET
IS
EVERYTHING

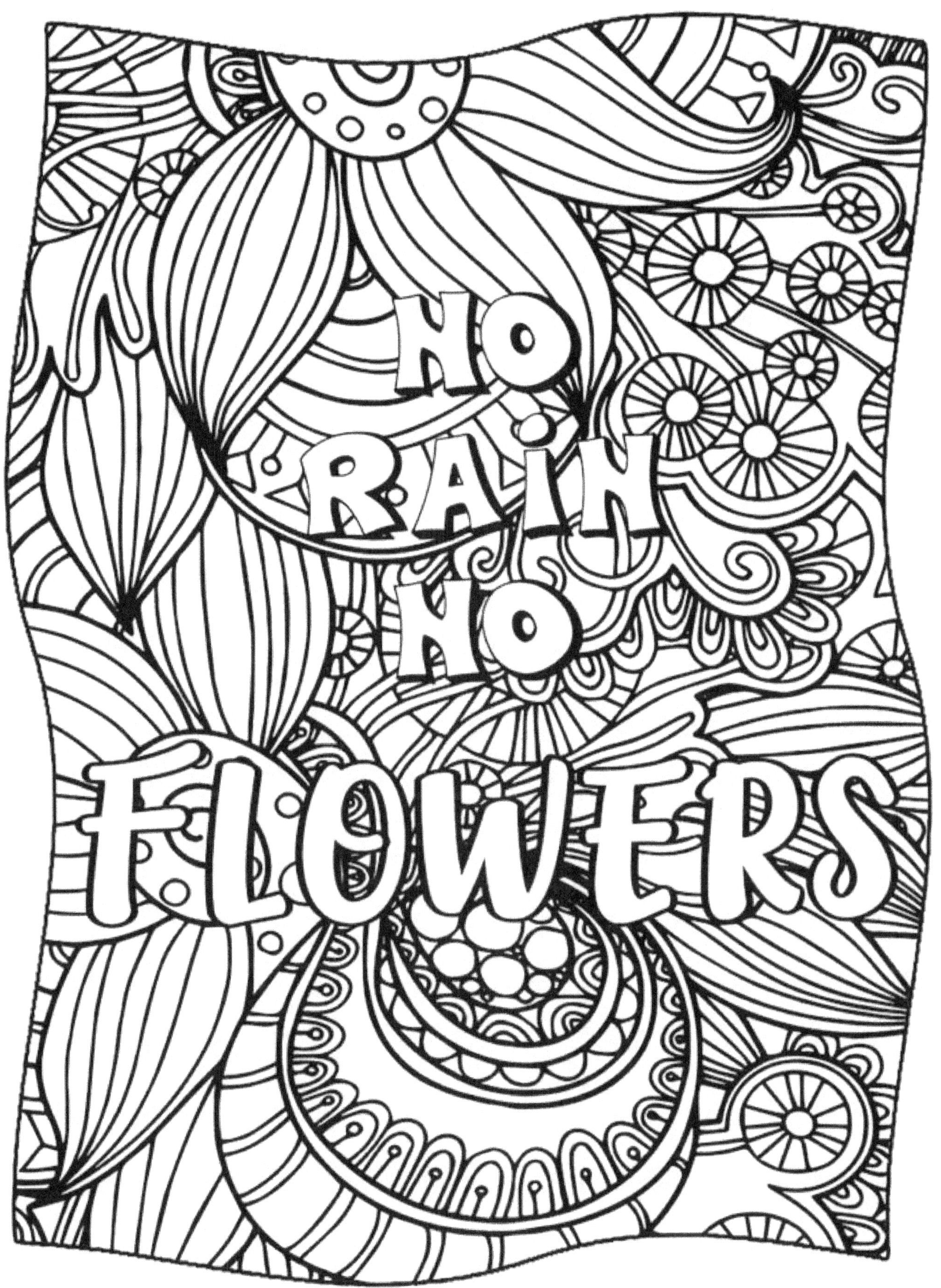

NO
RAIN
NO
FLOWERS

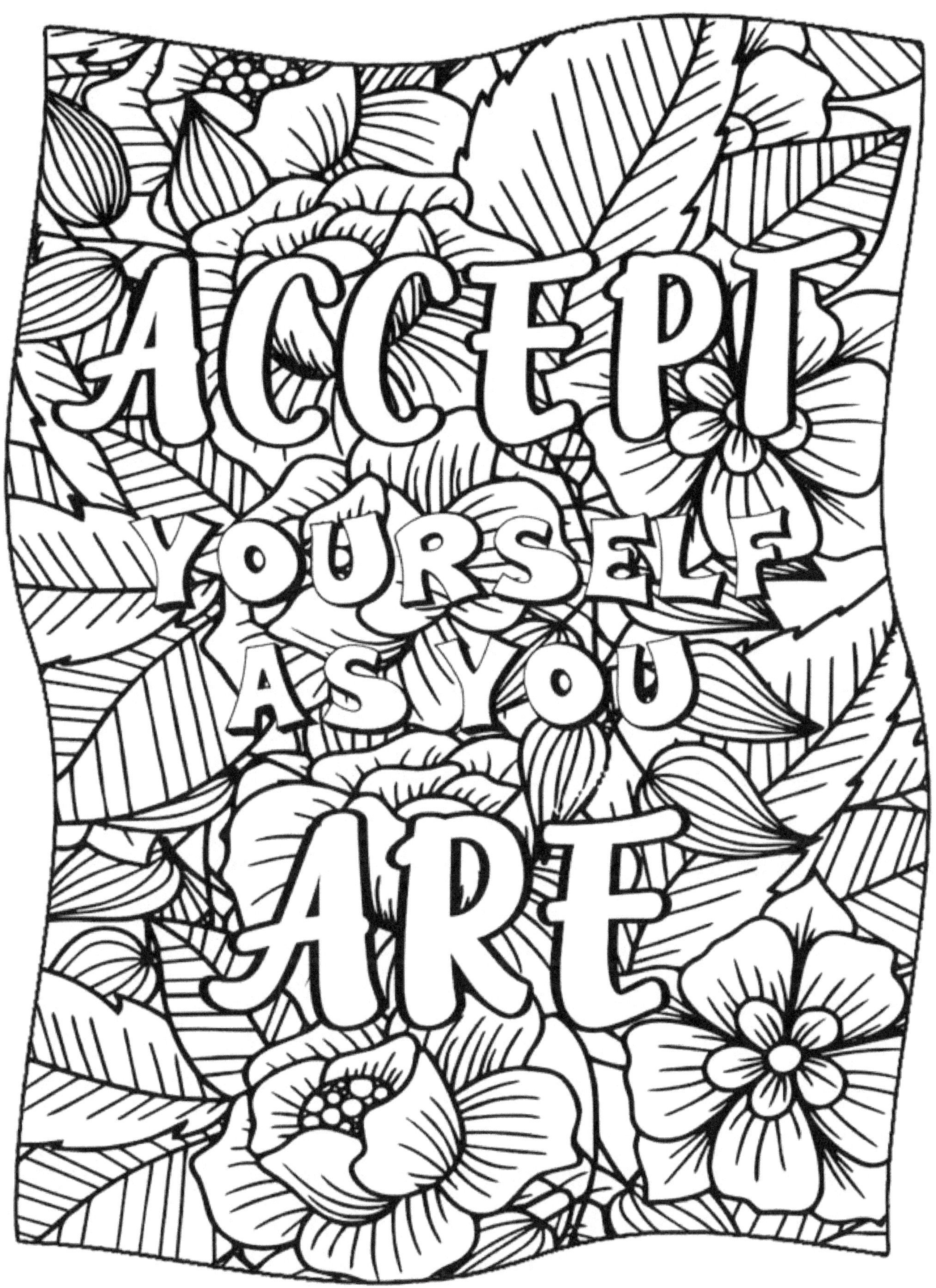

ACCEPT
YOURSELF
AS YOU
ARE

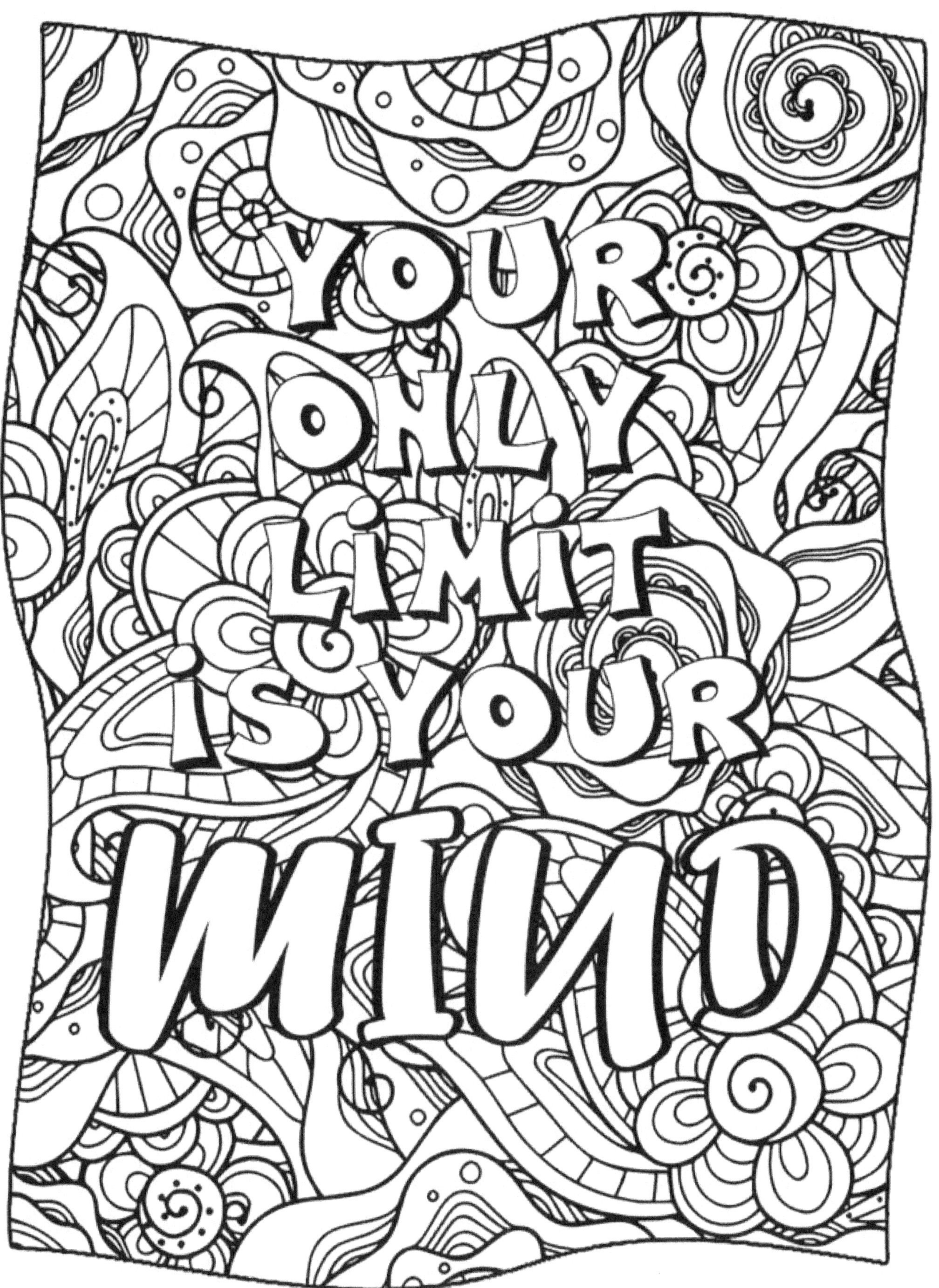

YOUR
ONLY
LIMIT
IS YOUR
MIND

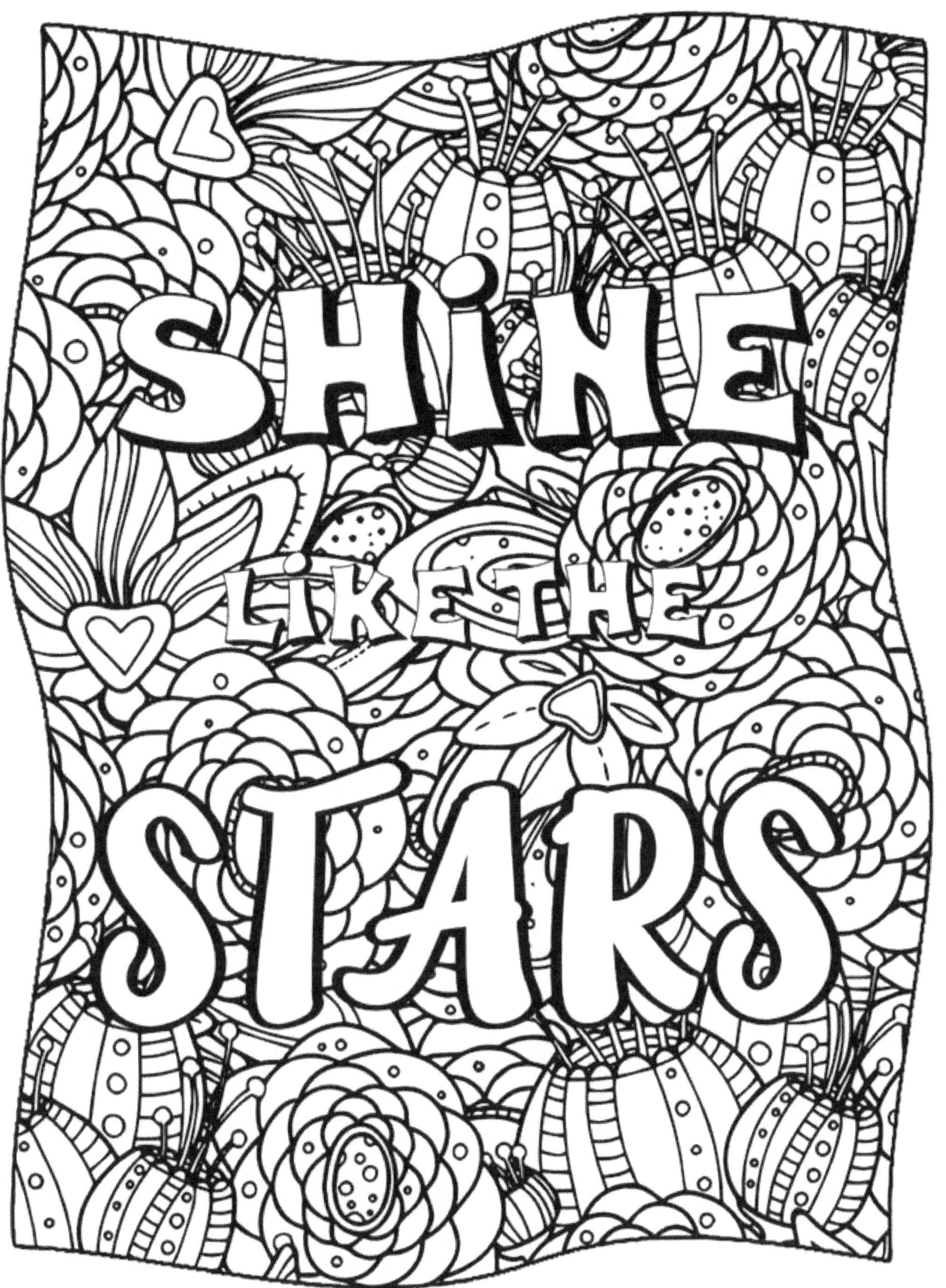

SHINE
LIKE THE
STARS